The busy woman's COOKBOOK

Ellen Sinclair
Food Editor

Soups hot and cold

Hot soups or cold are a tempting introduction to a meal. Or, with perhaps toasted sandwiches and salad to follow, they make a light satisfying meal in themselves.

Gourmet Chicken Soup

10 oz. can cream of chicken soup	1 tablespoon tarragon vinegar
½ pint water	½ cup cream
1 chicken stock cube	1 dessertspoon chopped parsley

Place soup, water, crumbled stock cube and vinegar in saucepan, stir over heat until well blended.

Bring just to boil, reduce heat, simmer 5 minutes. Stir in cream and parsley, heat gently.
Serves 4.

Oyster Soup

1 medium onion	1 dozen oysters
1 oz. butter	2 tablespoons instant mashed potato flakes
15 oz. can cream of mushroom soup	
1 cup milk	chopped parsley
2 rashers bacon	

Chop bacon, cook until crisp. Melt butter in saucepan, sauté chopped onion until transparent.

Stir in soup, milk, oysters with liquid and instant potato.

Simmer, stirring constantly, until hot.

Crumble a little bacon over each serving of soup. Sprinkle with chopped parsley.
Serves 4.

French Onion Soup

2 large onions	water
1 oz. butter	salt, pepper
2 15 oz. cans condensed beef consommé	

Peel onions, cut into thick slices.

Heat butter in pan, sauté onions until golden. Stir in consommé and one soup can of water. Season to taste with salt and pepper.

Bring to boil, reduce heat, simmer, covered, 20 minutes.

Pour into individual hot bowls or one large ovenproof dish. Toast slices of french bread, sprinkle well with grated parmesan cheese; grill to melt cheese a little. Place a toasted cheese slice on top of each bowl of soup.
Serves 6.
Note: A little rum, brandy or dry sherry added before bread is placed on top, gives a delicious flavour to soup.

Vegetable Chowder

4 rashers bacon	2 potatoes
1 large onion	3 cups milk
1 dessertspoon curry powder	10 oz. can whole kernel corn
2 15 oz. cans cream of celery soup	2 tablespoons chopped parsley
salt, pepper	

Peel potatoes, cut into dice, cook until tender, drain.

Dice bacon, cook gently in saucepan until crisp, remove from pan. Add chopped onion to bacon fat, cook gently until soft but not brown, stir in curry powder. Cook 2 minutes.

Add soup, milk, potatoes, corn with liquid from can and parsley.

Bring slowly to the boil, stirring constantly.

Season to taste with salt and pepper; add bacon just before serving.
Serves 6 to 8.

Sherried Mushroom Soup

2 oz. butter	¾ cup milk
4 oz. mushrooms	¾ cup water
salt, pepper	¼ cup dry sherry
15 oz. can cream of mushroom soup	

Melt butter in saucepan, add chopped mushrooms.

Sauté lightly 5 minutes. Add mushroom soup, stir until smooth; add salt and pepper.

Gradually stir in milk and water, continue stirring over low heat until almost boiling. Stir in sherry.
Serves 4.

Vichyssoise

2 oz. butter	3½ oz. packet instant
2 large onions	mashed potato
4 cups water	salt, pepper
3 chicken stock cubes	½ pint cream
2 cups milk	chopped chives or
	parsley

Melt butter in saucepan, add finely-chopped onions, cook until soft but not brown, add water and crumbled stock cubes, bring to boil.

Remove from heat, add 1 cup milk, stir in instant mashed potato powder, stir to blend. Add remaining milk, return to heat.

Cook, stirring, 5 minutes.

Remove from heat, add salt and pepper to taste and half the cream.

Refrigerate until well-chilled, stir in remaining cream. Sprinkle with chopped chives or parsley.

Serves 6.

Note: Traditionally, leeks are used in vichyssoise, but as they have a short season in Australia, onions are substituted. When they are available replace one of the onions with 2 leeks.

Creamy Tomato Soup

15 oz. can condensed	1 dessertspoon
tomato soup	tomato paste
1 cup water	¼ pint cream
1 chicken stock cube	chopped parsley
1 medium onion	

Combine soup, water, crumbled stock cube, chopped onion, and tomato paste in saucepan, heat gently, stirring until soup begins to boil.

Remove from heat, strain through sieve, stir in cream.

Refrigerate. Sprinkle a little chopped parsley over each serving.

Serves 4 to 6.

Chilled Mushroom Soup

15 oz. can cream of	¼ pint cream
mushroom soup	1 tablespoon dry white
water	wine
7 oz. can mushrooms	shallots
in butter sauce	

Combine soup with equal quantity of water, in saucepan, stir in undrained canned mushrooms. Bring to boil, stirring.

Remove from heat, cool slightly, stir in wine and cream.

Refrigerate. Serve sprinkled with finely-chopped shallots.

Serves 6.

Greek Egg and Lemon Soup

1 packet cream of	1 tablespoon lemon
chicken soup	juice
1 egg yolk	salt, pepper
	lemon slices

Prepare soup as directed on packet.

Simmer 15 minutes. Beat egg-yolk and lemon juice together in bowl.

Gradually add 1 cup soup, stirring steadily to prevent curdling.

Add this gradually to soup in saucepan, still stirring, cook 2 minutes.

Season to taste with salt and pepper.

Serve with lemon slices.

Serves 4.

Iced Borsch

1 cup sour cream	1 small onion
½ cup water	pinch sugar
1 chicken stock cube	salt, pepper
15 oz. can sliced	1 cup crushed ice
beetroot	chopped parsley
1 tablespoon lemon	
juice	

Place ¾ cup sour cream, water, crumbled stock cube, drained beetroot, lemon juice, sliced onion, sugar, in electric blender.

Blend on high speed 15 seconds; add salt and pepper to taste. Add crushed ice, blend further 10 seconds.

Serve immediately, topped with remaining sour cream, sprinkle with parsley.

Serves 4.

Avocado Soup

2 large ripe	1 cup sour cream
avocados	salt, pepper
1 dessertspoon	1 teaspoon
lemon juice	grated onion
2 15 oz. cans beef	chopped parsley
consommé or	
madrilene	

Halve avocados, scoop out flesh. Mash with lemon juice, or puree in blender approximately 12 seconds on low speed.

Warm soup slightly, remove from heat, combine with avocado, sour cream and onion.

Season with salt and pepper.

Refrigerate.

Top each serving with a little parsley.

Serves 6 to 8.

The First Course

First courses should be light, tempting the palate for the main courses to follow. Here we give suggestions and recipes for impressive first courses which can be prepared with a minimum of time and effort.

Hors d'Oeuvre

A selection of hors-d'oeuvre can be obtained from the delicatessen; thin slices of salami or continental sausage; black or green olives; slices of dill pickle; roll mops; anchovies; small canned mushrooms; artichoke hearts; tomato wedges; asparagus spears; canned salads. Arrange decoratively on large platter. Serve with thin slices of black, rye or pumpernickel bread.

The following are all appetising ways to begin a meal.

Canned asparagus with a little french dressing spooned over and sprinkled with parsley.

Canned artichoke hearts served in similar way.

Honeydew melon topped with a thin slice of ham.

Small triangles of buttered black bread served with canned smoked salmon.

Hard-boiled eggs halved, with mayonnaise spooned over, sprinkled with chopped parsley.

Halved grapefruit carefully separated from skin with a sharp knife and sprinkled with a teaspoon of sugar and a teaspoon of sherry.

Fresh Vegetable Dip

This is an unusual and delightfully fresh-tasting pre-dinner nibble. Use any fresh, crunchy vegetables in season. Suitable vegetables are small flowerets of white cauliflower, sliced zucchinis, sliced baby carrots, radishes, celery, red or green pepper strips. Wash them well, store in plastic bag in refrigerator to crisp. This can be done the night before, with the exception of the zucchinis and carrots; do these the night of the party, drop them into iced water, refrigerate until serving time.

Cheese Wine Dip: Blend together thoroughly the contents of an 8 oz. jar cheese spread and 2 tablespoons madeira (or dry white or red wine).

Spoon into small bowl. This can also be prepared the night before; cover with plastic food wrap before refrigerating.

Place the cheese dip in centre of plate, tray, or platter; arrange vegetables round.

This is finger-food; guests take a piece of crisp vegetable and dip it into the Cheese Wine dip. *Note*: Any favourite dip can be used in place of the Cheese Wine Dip.

Asparagus Mornay

Heat 2 10 oz. cans asparagus in their liquid. Make up 1 packet cheese sauce mix according to directions on packet.

Arrange drained asparagus on serving plates, spoon sauce over.

Sprinkle with toasted slivered almonds.

Mushrooms à la Greque

½ cup oil	1 bayleaf
½ cup white vinegar	2 cloves garlic
½ lb. mushrooms	chopped parsley
salt, pepper	

Slice mushrooms thickly, or leave whole if small.

Heat oil in a saucepan, add mushrooms, sauté 5 minutes.

Add vinegar, crushed garlic and seasonings.

Simmer, uncovered, 10 to 15 minutes.

Remove bayleaf. Pour into serving dish.

Refrigerate before serving.

Serve sprinkled with chopped parsley.

Serve 2 to 3.

Antipasto Salad takes only minutes to prepare, makes a perfect first course: salami slices, black olives, asparagus spears, roll mops (from the delicatessen), topped with thin onion slices; small canned whole mushrooms; cucumber slices and tomato wedges.

Avocado Vinaigrette

Cut avocados in half, remove stone. Score the inside of avocados criss-cross fashion, just down to the skin, as this enables flavour of dressing to penetrate. Spoon over a little french dressing.

Avocado with Smoked Oysters

2 ripe avocados	4 oz. can smoked oysters
2 tablespoons dry vermouth	1 tablespoon lemon juice

Halve avocados, remove stones, carefully scoop out flesh, keeping it in one piece as much as possible. Cut in slices with stainless steel knife, place in bowl.

Drain smoked oysters, mix with lemon juice; add to avocado slices. Add vermouth, mix lightly, taking care not to break slices. Fill avocado shells with mixture.

Serve on lettuce with small wedges of lemon. Serves 4.

Avocado Slices with Ham

2 ripe avocados	french dressing
lemon juice	½ lb. proscuitto ham

Peel avocados, remove stones. Slice with stainless steel knife, brush with lemon juice. Arrange slices on individual serving dishes, sprinkle with french dressing. Arrange ham slices beside or over avocado.

Proscuitto is raw Italian ham, available at large food stores. However, if not available, thin slices of lean ham can be substituted.

Serves 4.

Vegetable Cocktail

1 stick celery	1 tablespoon lemon juice
1 carrot	
3 sprigs parsley	1 teaspoon worcester-shire sauce
15 oz. can tomato juice	½ teaspoon salt

Chop vegetables roughly, combine in blender with all other ingredients.

Blend on high speed 30 seconds. Pour into glasses, garnish with slice of lemon.

Serves 4.

To make an excellent soup, add another 15 oz. can tomato juice to above mixture. Serve well chilled.

To serve as a hot soup: combine all ingredients, bring just to boiling point.

The vegetables will still be crisp and lightly crunchy.

Stuffed Eggs

Eggs, hard-boiled and halved, with yolks removed and combined with savoury ingredients, make a delicious snack or first course.

Hard-boil eggs, cool and shell. Cut in halves lengthwise, remove yolks.

Rub yolks through sieve, using wooden spoon, then mix in any of following well-blended combinations and spoon or pipe back into egg-halves.

Quantities given are sufficient for 6 eggs, unless otherwise stated.

1½ oz. jar black caviar, ¾ cup cream, salt, pepper, 1 teaspoon lemon juice. (Sufficient for 12 eggs.)

2 tablespoons finely-chopped ham, 2 chopped gherkins, salt, pepper. Add sufficient mayonnaise to make a creamy mixture.

2 tablespoons paté, 1 tablespoon chopped parsley, salt and pepper.

2 tablespoons cream cheese, 1 teaspoon anchovy paste, salt and pepper. Add mayonnaise to make a creamy mixture.

¼ cup canned tuna, 1 teaspoon prepared mustard, salt, pepper, mayonnaise to bind. Decorate plate with black olives.

1½ oz. can anchovies. Chop finely, add to yolks with sufficient mayonnaise to bind.

Stuffed Mushrooms

½ lb. small mushrooms	1 dessertspoon chopped parsley
2 oz. butter	2 tablespoons fresh breadcrumbs, melted butter
1 small clove garlic	
salt, pepper	
3 shallots	
1 rasher bacon	

Remove stems from wiped mushrooms; chop stems finely. Remove rind from bacon; chop bacon finely.

Melt butter in pan, add chopped bacon and mushroom stems.

Sauté with crushed garlic 2 minutes. Add salt and pepper to taste, parsley, and chopped shallots.

Cook gently 1 minute.

Remove from heat, add breadcrumbs.

Fill mushroom caps with this mixture. Place in shallow, well-greased ovenproof dish, pour 1 teaspoon melted butter or oil over each mushroom.

Bake in moderate oven 10 to 15 minutes.

Salmon Mousse

1 egg	1/3 cup oil, approx.
1/2 teaspoon dry mustard	8 oz. can red salmon
salt, pepper	1/4 pint cream
pinch sugar	2 teaspoons gelatine
1 tablespoon lemon juice	2 tablespoons boiling water

Place pepper, salt, mustard, sugar and egg in blender. Blend few seconds on low speed, add lemon juice.

With blender on, slowly pour in oil. The sound of the blender will be noticed to change when about 1/3 cup oil has been added. When this happens, mayonnaise is ready for use.

Dissolve gelatine in the boiling water. Add to mayonnaise in blender and, with blender still working, add undrained salmon, and cream. When all are smoothy blended, pour into serving dish or bowl.

Refrigerate until set. Serve cucumber salad separately.

Serves 4.

Oysters Kilpatrick

Season oysters on the half-shell with a few drops of worcestershire sauce, salt and pepper. Cover each oyster with 1 or 2 small strips of bacon.

Place under hot griller until bacon is crisp.

Oysters Rockefeller

Cover oysters on the half-shell with mixture of finely chopped, cooked spinach, grated onion and few drops of lemon juice.

Top with breadcrumbs and finely grated cheese. Brown under hot griller.

Quick Paté with Caviar

1 lb. best liverwurst	1 1/2 oz. jar caviar
2 tablespoons cream	(red or black)
1 tablespoon brandy	

Skin liverwurst, mash with cream and brandy. Spoon into serving bowl, spread caviar evenly across top.

Seafood Waldorf Salad

1 lb. shelled prawns	mayonnaise
1/4 cup chopped walnuts	salt, pepper
2 red apples	lettuce leaves

Wash apples, dry, cut into cubes (do not peel).

Combine prawns, apples and nuts; season with salt and pepper. Add sufficient mayonnaise to coat lightly; if desired, add a good squeeze of lemon juice to mayonnaise for extra flavour.

Serve on leaves of crisp lettuce.

Serves 2 to 3.

Salmon with Mayonnaise

Drain and bone 8 oz. can of red salmon; keep salmon in as large pieces as possible.

Arrange crisp lettuce on 2 plates, top with salmon.

Spoon over mayonnaise. Flavoured mayonnaise curry, dill, etc. are available. These can be used in place of the plain mayonnaise or add a little curry powder or dill to plain mayonnaise.

Serve with cucumber slices: remove skin, score sides with fork, cut cucumber in thin slices; put in small bowl, spoon over 1 tablespoon white vinegar, pinch salt, pinch sugar, stand 10 to 15 minutes.

Drain well before serving.

Serves 2.

Consommé and Sour Cream

Empty 2 15 oz cans beef consommé into large shallow bowl.

Freeze 20 minutes to speed up jelling, transfer to main part of refrigerator until ready to serve.

To serve, spoon jellied consommé into four bowls, top with a spoonful of sour cream and a spoonful of caviar, if desired.

Or consommé can be gently heated, just until it is liquid; stir in 2 tablespoons dry sherry. Refrigerate until jellied.

Top each serving with a spoonful of sour cream.

Serves 4.

Salads

Salads are not only for summer; they make a fresh, colourful addition to meals throughout the year. Here are recipes to serve with grills, for dinner party or buffet tables, for barbecues.

Green Salads

A small green side salad is an ideal accompaniment to many dishes. Lettuce alone makes the true green salad, but you might like to add slices of avocado, lightly brushed with lemon juice to retain the colour, or slices of green pepper or sliced canned artichoke hearts. Black or green olives are also a good addition.

Wash lettuce well, dry thoroughly. Put into plastic bag and refrigerate at least an hour to crisp.

To make french dressing: Use 3 parts of oil to 1 of vinegar, or equal quantities of oil and vinegar, depending on taste, (or use bottled french dressing). Add salt, pepper, a little dry or prepared mustard, a pinch of paprika.

Combine all ingredients in screw-top jar, shake well to combine.

Add crushed garlic if you like a garlic-flavoured dressing; not too much—the garlic flavour will become very pronounced if the dressing has to stand before use.

When ready to serve, tear lettuce roughly, put into bowl, sprinkle over the dressing—not a lot, just enough to coat leaves well.

There should not be any surplus dressing at base of bowl after salad is mixed. Toss salad lightly to give leaves a glossy coating of dressing.

Curried Rice Salad

¾ lb. long grain rice
8 shallots
1 green pepper
2 oz. toasted
  slivered almonds
1 dessertspoon
  curry powder
¾ cup french dressing
salt

Cook rice in usual way until tender, drain and cool. Chop shallots into 1 in. pieces, cut pepper into thin strips. Add shallots, pepper, and almonds to rice. Blend curry powder with dressing, add to rice mixture, season to taste with salt; toss well.
Serves 6.

Asparagus Rice Salad

½ lb. long grain rice
1 large onion
1 oz. butter
10 oz. can
  asparagus tips
2 tablespoons
  chopped parsley
2 tablespoons french
  dressing
salt, pepper

Cook rice in usual way, drain and cool. Heat butter in saucepan, add chopped onion, sauté until soft but not brown. Drain asparagus, discard liquid. Add onion, asparagus, parsley and dressing to rice; season with salt and pepper to taste, toss lightly.
Serves 4.

Tomatoes with Black Olives

3 tomatoes
1 large white onion
1 small cucumber
1 green pepper
2-3 tablespoons
  french dressing
pinch sugar
2 oz. black olives
salt, pepper
lettuce

Peel cucumber, cut into thin slices, place in bowl with 1 tablespoon of the dressing, and sugar, stand 15 minutes, drain.

Arrange lettuce leaves on serving plate, arrange in layers the skinned, sliced tomatoes, sliced onion and cucumber; top with green pepper rings. Season well with salt and pepper, spoon remaining dressing over. Garnish with black olives.
Serves 4.

Zucchini Salad

6 zucchini
2 oz. butter
4 sticks celery
¼ cup french dressing

Slice washed, unpeeled zucchini thinly; chop celery. Heat butter, add vegetables, sauté 2 minutes. Add french dressing, mix well. Serve warm or refrigerate until cold. Sprinkle with chopped parsley or a little finely-chopped mint.
Serves 4.

Mushroom and Spinach Salad—choose very young, tender spinach for this delicious salad, the perfect accompaniment to grills. (See page 13.)

Potato and Cucumber Salad

2 lb. potatoes	4 shallots
boiling salted water	¾ cup mayonnaise
1 medium cucumber	salt, pepper
1 teaspoon vinegar	lettuce leaves

Peel potatoes, cut into dice. Cook in boiling salted water until tender. Score washed, unpeeled cucumber with fork, cut in half lengthwise, slice thinly: chop shallots. Combine prepared vegetables in large bowl.

Combine mayonnaise, vinegar, salt and pepper, spoon over salad, toss lightly. Refrigerate.

To serve, spoon into lettuce-lined bowl.

Serves 6.

Potato and Egg Salad

1 lb. potatoes	¼ teaspoon paprika
4 shallots	4 eggs
½ cup french	1 tablespoon
dressing	chopped parsley
lettuce	extra french dressing

Chop shallots. Cook potatoes in boiling salted water until barely tender, peel and slice thickly while still hot. Place in bowl, add dressing, toss lightly. Allow to stand at room temperature 30 minutes while potatoes absorb dressing.

Hard-boil eggs, cool and peel; cut into wedges or slices, sprinkle with a little extra french dressing.

Add paprika and parsley to potatoes, stir in carefully. Serve on lettuce leaves, arrange eggs on top, spoon over any dressing that was not absorbed into potatoes. Sprinkle with chopped shallots.

Serves 4.

Curried Potato Salad

½ cup mayonnaise	2 lb. potatoes
¼ cup french dressing	salt
1 dessertspoon sugar	1 medium onion
1½ teaspoons curry	6 sticks celery
powder	lettuce

Peel potatoes, cut into cubes. Cook in boiling salted water until tender. In a bowl blend mayonnaise, french dressing, sugar, curry powder and salt; add finely chopped onion, sliced celery and potatoes, toss lightly.

Refrigerate, serve on crisp lettuce.

Serves 6.

Italian Onion Salad

3 large white onions	2 tablespoons red
1 large red pepper	wine
½ teaspoon salt	¾ teaspoon salt,
water	extra
¼ cup oil	¼ teaspoon oregano
½ small clove garlic	¼ cup finely chopped
pepper	parsley
	lettuce

Peel and slice onions, place in saucepan, cover with cold water, add ½ teaspoon salt, bring to boil, drain immediately. Add red pepper which has been seeded and cut into rings, for last 5 minutes of cooking; drain and cool. In screw-top jar combine oil, crushed garlic, wine, extra salt, oregano and pepper.

Shake dressing vigorously before serving, pour over vegetables. Serve on crisp lettuce leaves sprinkled with parsley.

Serves 4.

Tomato and Onion Salad

4 tomatoes	1 white onion
salt, pepper	1 tablespoon chopped
¼ cup french	parsley or chives
dressing	

Peel tomatoes, cut into thick slices; slice onion. Place tomatoes in shallow dish, sprinkle with salt and pepper. Cover with onion slices, spoon over dressing. Sprinkle with chopped parsley or chives before serving.

Serves 4.

Artichoke Green Salad

15 oz. can artichoke	4 shallots
hearts	2 tablespoons
3 sticks celery	chopped parsley
1 lettuce	1 cucumber
1 green pepper	½ cup french dressing

Cut artichoke hearts in half, if they are large. Slice celery, green pepper, shallots and cucumber, shred lettuce. Combine in bowl with artichoke hearts, parsley and dressing, toss lightly.

Serves 4.

Salami and Olive Salad

¼ firm cabbage	1 green pepper
¼ lb. salami in one piece	¼ cup mayonnaise
6 shallots	¼ cup french dressing
2 oz. green or black olives	salt, pepper

Shred cabbage, wash and drain well. Chop salami into ½ in. cubes, chop shallots and pepper. Put cabbage, salami, shallots, pepper and olives in salad bowl. Combine mayonnaise, dressing, salt and pepper, pour over salad, toss well.
Serves 4.

Caesar Salad

2 small lettuce	2 rashers bacon
1 oz. butter	1 tablespoon grated parmesan cheese
1 clove garlic	chopped parsley
2 slices bread	

Dressing:

⅔ cup french dressing	1 coddled egg
1 teaspoon salt	1 teaspoon prepared mustard

Wash lettuce well, dry, refrigerate until crisp. Tear leaves into pieces, mix with dressing. Cut bread into ¼ in. cubes. Brown cubes with crushed garlic in hot butter. Cook chopped bacon separately until crisp, drain on absorbent paper. Scatter bread croutons over salad with bacon pieces, chopped parsley and cheese; toss lightly.
Dressing: Coddle egg by lowering gently into boiling water and boiling 1 minute. Remove shell; combine with remaining ingredients. Blend well.
Serves 4 to 6.

Blue Cheese Salad

½ cup french dressing	4 sticks celery
1 small clove garlic	1 onion
1 small lettuce	3 medium tomatoes
1 small green pepper	4 oz. blue cheese
salt, pepper	

Combine crushed garlic and dressing, place in bowl. Tear washed, crisped lettuce into small pieces, combine in bowl with chopped green pepper, chopped celery, chopped onion, salt, pepper; toss lightly. Cut skinned tomatoes into quarters, add just before serving. Top with crumbled blue cheese.
Serves 4 to 6.

Mushroom and Spinach Salad

1 lb. fresh mushrooms	2 tablespoons chopped parsley
½ clove garlic	1 tablespoon lemon juice
oil	salt, pepper
1 bunch young spinach	
¼ cup french dressing	

Wash mushrooms, pat dry, trim off hard ends of stalks; slice thickly. Spoon over just enough oil to moisten; mix lightly, stand 5 minutes. Add parsley, lemon juice and salt and pepper, stir to combine, stand 10 minutes. Tear spinach into small pieces, place in separate bowl, add dressing, to which crushed garlic has been added; toss lightly. Add to mushrooms, mix together gently.
Serves 6.

Coleslaw

½ medium cabbage	6 shallots
2 carrots	4 sticks celery

Dressing:

1 tablespoon lemon juice	½ teaspoon dry mustard
¾ cup mayonnaise	salt, pepper

Remove stalk and shred cabbage very finely; grate carrots. Cut celery and shallots, including green tops, into diagonal pieces. Mix together all prepared vegetables and add enough dressing to give even coating. Mix well.
Dressing: Place all dressing ingredients in small basin, mix well.
Serves 4 to 6.

Haricot Bean Salad

1 lb. haricot beans	½ cup french dressing
boiling salted water	½ cup chopped parsley
2 oz. green olives	salt, pepper
1 clove garlic	

Cover beans well with water, allow to stand overnight. Drain, add to large saucepan of boiling salted water, boil 1 to 1½ hours or until tender, drain well; allow to become cold. Pit and slice green olives, add to beans with crushed garlic, dressing and parsley. Season with salt and pepper, toss lightly to combine.
Refrigerate before serving.
Serves 6.

Fish

Fish—fresh, quick-frozen or canned—can be transformed into delicious and interesting meals for all occasions.

Fish Fingers in Sauce Verte

1 large packet quick-frozen fish fingers	salt, pepper
	¼ cup mayonnaise
10 oz. packet quick-frozen chopped spinach	1 tablespoon white wine
	1 teaspoon lemon juice

Place frozen fish fingers on greased oven tray.
Bake in moderate oven 20 minutes.
Cook spinach according to directions on packet.
Combine mayonnaise, wine and lemon juice, mix until smooth, season to taste with salt and pepper.
Stir in undrained spinach, blend well.
Serve sauce with fish fingers.
Serves 4.

Tuna à la King

2 oz. small mushrooms	2 chicken stock cubes
1 small green pepper	salt, pepper
2 oz. butter	¼ pint cream
¼ cup flour	7 to 8 oz. can tuna
1½ cups hot water	

Slice mushrooms. Remove seeds and dice pepper.
Melt butter in pan, add mushrooms and green pepper.
Cook gently 3 minutes.
Remove from pan.
Add flour to pan-drippings, cook 1 minute.
Remove from heat, gradually add hot water; add stock cubes.
Return to heat, bring to boil, stirring; reduce heat, stirring until smooth and thickened.
Season to taste with salt and pepper.
Add cream, drained tuna and vegetables, heat gently.
Serve with hot rice.
Serves 4.

Crab Creole

7 to 8 oz. can crabmeat	¼ cup water
	¼ cup chopped parsley
15 oz. can whole tomatoes	1 large green pepper
3 medium onions	3 sticks celery
1 tablespoon paprika	salt, pepper
2 tablespoons tomato paste	

Remove fibres from crabmeat.
Peel onions, chop finely. Remove seeds from green pepper, dice.
Wash and slice celery finely.
Pour undrained tomatoes into pan, crush tomatoes with fork or potato masher; add all remaining ingredients, except crabmeat. Bring slowly to boil; reduce heat, cover.
Simmer 10 minutes.
Stir in crabmeat, reheat gently.
Serve with hot rice.
Serves 4.
Note: Prawns can be used in place of, or in addition to, the crabmeat.

Garlic Prawns

For one serving:

5 green king prawns	2 tablespoons oil, or
4 cloves garlic	2 oz. butter
1 small chilli	

Place oil or butter in small ovenproof dish; heat until sizzling.
Add crushed garlic, halved chilli and shelled prawns.
Cook in moderately hot oven until prawns turn pink.
Serve at once, while oil is still sizzling.
Note: In place of the chilli, few drops of hot chilli sauce can be added to the oil.

Fish Fillets in Tomato Sauce, deliciously seasoned fish casserole in a rich, colourful sauce. (See page 16.)

Easy Fish Pie

2 cups fresh white breadcrumbs	2 oz. butter
1 large onion	salt, pepper
3 medium tomatoes	½ teaspoon curry powder
½ lb. fish fillets	

Peel and chop onion finely.

Sauté in 1 oz. of the butter with curry powder 4 minutes.

Skin and bone fillets, cut into bite-size pieces.

Place one-third of breadcrumbs in greased pie dish, cover with half the onion mixture, then half the skinned, sliced tomatoes. Sprinkle with salt and pepper.

Place fish pieces on top. Repeat layers of breadcrumbs, onion, tomato, salt and pepper; top with remaining breadcrumbs, dot with remaining butter.

Bake in moderate oven 40 to 45 minutes.

Serves 4.

Baked Fish Fillets in Tomato Sauce

1½ lb. fish fillets	1 chicken stock cube
flour	1 dessertspoon lemon juice
1 cup hot water	
2 tablespoons tomato paste	4 shallots
	salt, pepper

Skin and bone fillets, toss in flour seasoned with salt and pepper. Put fillets into ovenproof dish. Combine water, tomato paste, crumbled stock cube, and lemon juice in bowl, add chopped shallots; season to taste with salt and pepper.

Pour over fish, cover.

Bake in moderate oven 30 minutes.

Serves 4.

Fish Meunière

1½ lb. fish fillets	1½ tablespoons lemon juice
flour	
salt, pepper	lemon slices
4 oz. butter	chopped parsley

Skin and bone fillets. Cut fillets into serving-size pieces, toss lightly in flour seasoned with salt and pepper.

Melt 3 oz. butter in pan, fry fillets until brown on both sides; remove from pan.

Melt remaining butter in pan; add lemon juice, spoon over fish.

Serve sprinkled with chopped parsley, decorate with lemon slices.

Serves 4.

Baked Fish Fillets with Caper Sauce

1½ lb. fish fillets	2 anchovy fillets
1 medium onion	salt, pepper
1 bayleaf	½ teaspoon vinegar
1 teaspoon lemon juice	1 tablespoon drained capers
¼ cup water	1 tablespoon chopped parsley
4 oz. butter	

Skin and bone fillets, fold in half and place in ovenproof dish with sliced onion, bayleaf, lemon juice and water.

Bake, covered, in moderate oven 20 minutes.

Drain fillets, transfer to serving dish; keep warm. Melt butter in pan, add chopped anchovy fillets.

Heat and stir without letting butter boil.

Add remaining ingredients; spoon over fish fillets.

Serves 4.

Prawn Cocktail

1½ lb. prawns	lemon slices
lettuce	

Sauce:

3 tablespoons mayonnaise	4 tablespoons lightly whipped cream
3 tablespoons tomato sauce	few drops tabasco sauce
1 tablespoon brandy	salt, pepper
1 dessertspoon worcestershire sauce	

Shell prawns, reserve 6 large ones for garnishing. Wash lettuce, tear into small pieces, or shred finely.

Arrange lettuce over base of 6 serving glasses. Top with prawns, spoon over sauce.

Garnish each glass with lemon slice and reserved prawns.

Sauce: Combine mayonnaise, tomato sauce, brandy and worcestershire sauce in basin, lightly stir in cream; season to taste with tabasco sauce, salt and pepper.

Serves 6.

Tuna Casserole

¾ cup coarsely crushed potato crisps	water
	1 onion
	3 sticks celery
3 tablespoons oil	¼ cup lemon juice
15 oz. can tuna	2 oz. salted cashews
10 oz. can cream of celery soup	salt, pepper

Heat oil in frying pan, add chopped onion and sliced celery.

Sauté until almost tender.

Remove from pan.

Mix together undrained tuna, soup, the soup can half-full of water, lemon juice, cashews, salt and pepper. Add onion and celery.

Transfer to greased ovenproof dish.

Bake, uncovered, in moderate oven 20 minutes.

Remove, top with crushed potato chips, return to moderate oven further 15 minutes.

Serves 4.

Sherried Fish Fillets

1½ lb. fish fillets	2 oz. butter
4 tablespoons dry sherry	1 tablespoon chopped parsley
4 tablespoons tomato sauce	1 teaspoon lemon juice
1 cup fresh bread-crumbs	salt, pepper

Skin and bone fillets, fold each in half. Place in greased ovenproof dish.

Spoon 3 tablespoons of sherry over fish, then spread with tomato sauce.

Melt butter in pan, add breadcrumbs, parsley, lemon juice, salt and pepper. Crumble bread-crumb mixture over fish, sprinkle with remaining sherry.

Bake, uncovered, in moderate oven 20 minutes.
Serves 4.

Baked Salmon Loaf

1 lb. can salmon	1 medium onion, chopped
10¾ oz. can con-densed vegetable soup	2 eggs
	salt, pepper
1 cup dry bread-crumbs	¼ cup chopped parsley

Combine all ingredients including salmon liquid, in bowl, mix well together.

Press mixture into greased 8 in. x 4 in. loaf tin.

Bake in moderate oven 30 minutes.

Serve hot or cold with salad.

Serves 4.

Salmon Mornay

15 to 16 oz. can salmon	½ cup grated cheese
	salt, pepper
1½ cups milk	1 teaspoon lemon juice
1½ oz. butter	2 tablespoons dry breadcrumbs
2 tablespoons flour	
1 chicken stock cube	1 oz. butter, extra

Drain and flake salmon; add water to salmon liquid to make ½ cup liquid.

Melt butter in pan, stir in flour.

Cook 1 minute. Remove from heat.

Gradually add milk and salmon liquid, blend well.

Return to heat, bring to boil, stirring; reduce heat, cook, stirring until smooth and thickened.

Stir in crumbled stock cube and grated cheese, leaving approximately 2 tablespoons of cheese for topping.

Add lemon juice and salt and pepper to taste. Fold in salmon.

Spoon mixture into ovenproof dish, top with breadcrumbs and remaining cheese, dot with extra butter.

Brown under hot griller or in hot oven.
Serves 3.

Hot Salmon Puffs

1 lb. packaged puff pastry	salt, pepper
	⅓ cup cream
7 or 8 oz. can red salmon	1 egg
4 shallots	

Drain, skin, and bone salmon. Put in saucepan with finely chopped shallots and cream. Cook, stirring, a few minutes until thickened. Season with salt and pepper; let stand until cold.

Roll out pastry to 18 in. x 12 in. rectangle, cut into 3 in. squares. Put a teaspoonful of salmon mixture in centre of each square. Wet along two edges, fold into triangle shape, press edges firmly together. Put on lightly greased oven trays. Brush well with beaten egg. Bake in hot oven 8 to 10 minutes until golden brown.

Makes approx. 2 dozen.

Sauces for Pastas

Spaghetti, with a deliciously savoury sauce, is a popular dish with all ages. Some of the sauces given here need only a short cooking time, some can be prepared ahead and just reheated before serving. One pound of spaghetti will give six servings.

Curried Steak Sauce

1½ lb. minced steak	3 tablespoons tomato
2 medium onions	paste
2 tablespoons curry	2¾ cups boiling
powder	water
2 teaspoons mixed	1 cup coconut
herbs	salt, pepper
	2 chicken stock cubes

Place minced steak in saucepan, stir until meat is well browned. Add chopped onions, cook 5 minutes. Add curry powder, mixed herbs, and tomato paste, cook, stirring a few minutes. Pour boiling water over coconut, leave 15 minutes, then strain, pressing coconut with spoon to get as much flavour as possible into the liquid. Discard coconut. Stir coconut milk into curry. Add crumbled stock cubes.

Bring to boil, reduce heat, simmer 25 minutes. Season to taste with salt and pepper. Spoon over hot spaghetti.

Serves 6.

Bolognese Sauce

1 large onion	salt, pepper
1 lb. minced steak	2 beef stock cubes
2 tablespoons oil	¼ teaspoon oregano
8 oz. can tomato paste	¼ teaspoon thyme
1 pint water	grated parmesan cheese

Sauté chopped onion in heated oil until golden, add minced steak; cook very well, stirring with fork all the time, until steak browns well. Pour off any surplus fat, add water, tomato paste, crumbled stock cubes, salt and pepper to taste, and herbs. Bring to boil, reduce heat, cook gently 1 to 1½ hours, uncovered, adding a little more water if sauce becomes thick too quickly. Serve over hot spaghetti.

Serve grated parmesan cheese separately.

Serves 4.

Note: This sauce can be prepared the day beforehand, refrigerated, and just reheated to serve. It also freezes well.

Marinara Sauce

1 oz. butter	1 chicken stock cube
1 clove garlic	½ lb. prawns
15 oz. can whole	½ lb. scallops
tomatoes	⅓ cup chopped
2 tablespoons tomato	parsley
paste	salt, pepper
½ cup water	

Melt butter in pan, sauté crushed garlic a few moments. Add tomatoes and liquid from can, tomato paste, water and crumbled stock cube. Crush tomatoes with fork or potato masher. Bring to boil, reduce heat, simmer, uncovered, 15 minutes. Add scallops and salt and pepper to taste, cook further 5 minutes. Add shelled prawns and parsley, cook further 5 minutes. Serves 4.

Italian Meat Balls

1 lb. minced steak	1 medium onion,
1 egg	finely chopped
¼ cup packaged dry	1 tablespoon chopped
breadcrumbs	parsley
1½ tablespoons	salt, pepper
grated parmesan	oil for frying
cheese	

Tomato Sauce:

1½ tablespoons oil	½ pint water
1 small onion	salt, pepper
5 oz. can tomato	
paste	

Combine all ingredients for meatballs in bowl; season to taste with salt and pepper, mix thoroughly. Shape into egg-sized balls. Fry in hot oil until evenly brown. Remove from pan and place in prepared sauce.

Bring to boil, reduce heat, simmer 30 minutes, uncovered. Spoon over hot spaghetti.

Tomato Sauce: Heat oil in saucepan. Cook finely chopped onion in oil until soft. Add tomato paste and water and stir until well blended. Season to taste with salt and pepper. Bring to boil, stirring constantly; reduce heat, add meatballs.

Simmer 30 minutes.

Serves 4.

Italian Meatballs—a tasty, filling dish suitable for the family or a savoury supper.

Chicken

Chicken is a popular dish for family meals, or for parties. The recipes given here offer a selection of quickly prepared dishes, or casseroles which can be prepared in advance.

Chicken in White Wine

2 whole chicken breasts	salt
flour	1 chicken stock cube
2 oz. butter	1 cup cream
1 cup dry white wine	1 dessertspoon brandy
	paprika

Remove bones from whole chicken breasts, flatten out, and cut each in two. Dust with flour seasoned with salt and pepper.

Melt butter in pan, sauté chicken gently about 5 minutes on each side.

Pour excess butter from pan, increase heat, and add wine.

Cook quickly until wine is reduced by half, then reduce heat, add cream, and cook gently, uncovered, until chicken is tender.

Add crumbled stock cube, brandy, and salt to taste.

Arrange on heated serving dishes, sprinkle with a little paprika.

Serves 2.

Chicken Newburg

2½-3 lb. chicken, steamed	¾ cup dry sherry
1 oz. butter	½ pint cream
salt, pepper	2 egg-yolks
	chopped parsley

Bone chicken, cut meat into large bite-size pieces.

Melt butter in pan.

Fry chicken pieces gently on both sides. Do not brown.

Sprinkle well with salt and pepper.

Pour sherry over, simmer slowly until almost all wine has reduced.

Beat together lightly egg-yolks and cream; pour over chicken, stir gently and shake pan over low heat until sauce thickens. Do not boil.

Sprinkle with parsley.

Serve with rice.

Serves 4.

Curry-Mayonnaise Chicken

6 chicken legs	1 cup packaged dry breadcrumbs
⅓ cup mayonnaise	
2 teaspoons curry powder	

Combine mayonnaise and curry powder, spread chicken legs with mixture. Coat with breadcrumbs, press on lightly with hands.

Place in well-greased baking dish.

Bake in moderate oven 45 minutes, or until tender.

Serves 3 or 6.

To prepare ahead: Prepare legs for baking, as described above, refrigerate.

Next day, bake as described.

Chicken with Asparagus

2 whole chicken breasts	1 tablespoon lemon juice
½ cup flour	10 oz. can asparagus tips
salt, pepper	chopped parsley
1 egg	1 tablespoon sweet vermouth
½ cup milk	¼ cup water
1½ cups fresh breadcrumbs	2 tablespoons cream
4 oz. butter	
¼ lb. mushrooms	

Cut breasts in half. Dust with seasoned flour, dip in combined egg and milk, coat with breadcrumbs.

Heat butter in frying pan, add chicken.

Fry on medium heat until golden brown on both sides; reduce heat, continue cooking until tender.

Add sliced mushrooms and lemon juice.

Heat asparagus separately in its liquid. Arrange chicken on serving plates, garnish with drained asparagus. Sprinkle with a little chopped parsley.

Add vermouth and water to pan drippings; stir well, stir in cream, salt and pepper heat gently.

Strain, serve with chicken.

Serves 4.

To prepare ahead: Coat chicken with crumbs, slice mushrooms.

Refrigerate, covered. Next day, proceed as above.

Pineapple Chicken

3 lb. chicken
  (or chicken pieces)
½ cup flour
salt, pepper
1 medium onion
1 green pepper

15 oz. can tomato
  soup
15 oz. can pineapple
  pieces
¾ cup water
1 chicken stock cube
2 oz. butter

Joint chicken. Dust chicken pieces with flour seasoned with salt and pepper.

Heat butter in large frying pan or large saucepan, add chicken pieces, fry until browned on all sides. Add sliced pepper and sliced onion.

Cook 2 minutes. Combine soup, undrained pineapple and water, add to chicken with crumbled stock cube.

Cover, cook slowly 40 to 50 minutes or until chicken is tender.

Serves 4.

To prepare ahead: Cook completly as above, reheat gently. Sliced pepper can be omitted in first cooking, and added when reheating.

Chicken Bordelaise

3 lb. chicken
  (or chicken pieces)
4 onions
6 oz. mushrooms
5 oz. butter
1 cup dry white wine
1 cup water
2 chicken stock cubes

salt, pepper
1 tablespoon tomato
  paste
¼ cup flour
1 cup water, extra
7 oz. can artichoke
  hearts
chopped parsley

Chop two of the onions finely, slice mushrooms. Melt 1 oz. butter in saucepan, sauté onions and mushrooms until lightly browned. Add wine, water and crumbled stock cubes, simmer until reduced to half quantity. Stir in tomato paste, season to taste with salt and pepper.

Cut chicken into serving size pieces. Melt 3 oz butter in separate saucepan, sauté chicken until brown on all sides, remove from pan. Add flour to pan, cook 1 minute. Remove from heat, gradually add extra water, blend well.

Add the mushroom sauce, return to heat, stir until sauce boils and thickens. Return chicken to pan, simmer, covered, until tender.

Cut remaining onions into thin slices, sauté in separate pan with drained artichoke hearts in remaining butter 5 minutes. Sprinkle chicken with chopped parsley, garnish with the onion rings and artichoke hearts.

Serves 4.

Lemon Chicken

3 lb. chicken
  (or chicken pieces)
½ cup flour

salt, pepper
2 teaspoons paprika
4 oz. butter

Lemon Sauce:

1 dessertspoon soy
  sauce
salt, pepper
¼ cup oil
⅓ cup lemon juice

1 dessertspoon
  grated lemon rind
1 clove garlic,
  crushed

Combine flour, salt, pepper and paprika. Cut chicken into serving-sized pieces; toss in the seasoned flour. Grease large ovenproof dish, arrange chicken pieces, skin-side down, in single layer. Melt butter, spoon over chicken. Bake uncovered, in hot oven 30 minutes, turn chicken, spoon Lemon Sauce over; cook further 30 minutes, or until tender, basting occasionally.

Lemon Sauce: Combine all ingredients, mix well.

Serves 4.

Apricot Chicken

3 lb. chicken pieces
1 packet onion soup
15 oz. can apricot
  nectar

1 teaspoon salt
¼ teaspoon pepper

Combine chicken pieces, onion soup, apricot nectar, salt and pepper in casserole dish. Cover, cook in a moderate oven 1½ hours or until chicken pieces are tender. Serve with rice.

Serves 4.

Chicken and Tomato Casserole

3 lb. chicken (or
  chicken pieces)
⅓ cup flour
3 oz. butter
2 onions
15 oz. can tomato
  juice

10 oz. can whole
  kernel corn, drained
¼ cup red wine
salt, pepper
chopped parsley

Cut chicken into serving-sized pieces, toss in flour. Heat butter in large pan, sauté chicken pieces until brown. Add peeled and chopped onions, sauté few minutes. Add all remaining ingredients, bring to boil, reduce heat, simmer, covered, 25 minutes or until tender. Serve sprinkled with chopped parsley.

Serves 4.

Curried Chicken Salad

3 lb. chicken, steamed	10½ oz. can asparagus pieces
15 oz. can whole mushrooms	1 red pepper
1 lettuce	½ cup french dressing
1 cucumber	2 teaspoons curry powder

Bone chicken, cut meat into small serving-sized pieces. Drain mushrooms and asparagus. Wash lettuce, dry well. Cut cucumber in half lengthwise, cut into slices. Cut pepper into thin strips. Combine chicken pieces with all vegetables except lettuce. Combine french dressing and curry powder, pour over salad, toss lightly. Arrange lettuce in salad bowl, spoon in the chicken salad.

Serves 4.

Whisky Chicken

4 whole chicken breasts	⅓ cup dry sherry
4 oz. butter	⅓ cup water
¼ cup whisky	1 chicken stock cube
1 red pepper	1 teaspoon lemon juice
½ pint cream	salt, pepper

Skin chicken breasts, cut in half, sauté in heated butter until brown, remove from pan. Add pepper, cut into thin strips, to pan drippings, sauté a few minutes, remove from pan. Add whisky to pan; when warmed, set aflame. Add cream, sherry, water, crumbled stock cube and lemon juice, blend well.

Return chicken and pepper to pan, simmer slowly, covered, until chicken is tender. Season to taste with salt and pepper.

Serves 4.

Garlic Lemon Chicken

4 chicken pieces	¼ cup lemon juice
1 teaspoon paprika	1 dessertspoon grated lemon rind
1 clove garlic	salt, pepper
1 dessertspoon soy sauce	

Place chicken pieces on large piece of aluminium foil. Combine crushed garlic with remaining ingredients, brush over chicken pieces. Wrap chicken tightly in the foil. Place in pan of simmering water, cover pan tightly, simmer gently 45 minutes to 1 hour, or until chicken is tender.

Serves 4.

Spaghetti with Chicken Livers

1 lb. chicken livers	¼ cup dry white wine
3 oz. butter	½ cup water
1 large onion	½ teaspoon mixed herbs
1 clove garlic	
4 oz. mushrooms	1 teaspoon salt
5 oz. can tomato paste	½ lb. spaghetti
15 oz. can whole tomatoes	

Clean chicken livers and cut into halves. Melt butter in pan, sauté chicken livers until lightly browned and tender, remove from pan. Add peeled and chopped onion, crushed garlic and sliced mushrooms to pan, sauté until tender.

Add tomatoes with juice (press with fork or potato masher to break up well), tomato paste, wine, water, herbs, and salt, stir to combine and simmer gently, covered, 20 minutes. Chop livers and return to pan and stir well.

Cook spaghetti in boiling salted water approximately 15 minutes, or until tender. Drain well and fold into sauce.

Serves 4.

Chinese Chicken

8 chicken legs	1 clove garlic
¼ cup brandy	½ teaspoon salt
1 tablespoon soy sauce	¼ teaspoon pepper
	oil for deep-frying

Prick chicken legs several times with skewer or a fine-tined fork, so that they can absorb the marinade.

Combine brandy, soy sauce, crushed garlic, salt and pepper in bowl; add chicken legs, marinate overnight or for several hours.

Heat oil in saucepan, add drained chicken legs, deep-fry 15 to 20 minutes, or until chicken legs are cooked through.

These are delicious served hot, or cold. They're good finger-food for a party; nice, too, to take along on a picnic, with salad.

Curried Chicken Salad—chicken, asparagus and colourful salad vegetables are tossed in a lightly curry-flavoured dressing.

Chicken Provencale

3 lb. chicken	1 clove garlic
(or chicken pieces)	½ cup dry sherry
¾ cup flour	15 oz. can tomato
salt, pepper	purée
4 oz. butter	2 oz. black olives
1 medium onion	chopped parsley

Joint chicken, dust with flour seasoned with salt and pepper.

Heat butter in frying pan, add chicken, sauté quickly until golden on all sides; transfer to casserole.

Add chopped onion and crushed garlic to remaining butter in frying pan, cook slowly until soft, but not brown.

Add sherry to pan, boil 1 minute, add tomato pureé, stir until boiling, add salt and pepper to taste, pour over chicken.

Cover, bake in moderate oven 1 hour, or until chicken is tender.

Add black olives and sprinkle with chopped parsley just before serving.

Serves 4.

To prepare ahead: Cook the entire dish, cool and refrigerate.

Next day, add olives; heat through in moderate oven.

Brandied Chicken

3 lb. chicken	1 teaspoon curry
(or chicken pieces)	powder
2 large onions	salt, pepper
3 oz. butter	¼ pint cream
1 tablespoon oil	1 tablespoon brandy

Joint chicken. Heat oil and butter in saucepan or deep frying pan, add sliced onions.

Cook until tender but not brown; stir in curry powder. Add chicken pieces, cover pan.

Simmer over gentle heat 30 minutes or until chicken is tender.

Add salt and pepper, stir in brandy and cream; heat gently.

Serves 4.

To prepare ahead: Cook as above, until chicken is tender.

Next day reheat gently, add brandy and cream.

Chicken Mornay

3 lb. chicken,	¼ cup sour cream
steamed	¼ cup dry white wine
2 oz. butter	½ a 10 oz. can whole
1 medium onion	kernel corn
2 sticks celery	7 oz. can whole
⅓ cup flour	mushrooms
1 cup milk	1½ oz. cheese
1 cup water	1 cup fresh
salt, pepper	breadcrumbs
1 chicken stock cube	1 oz. butter, extra

Remove meat from chicken, and cut into cubes. Heat butter in saucepan, add chopped onion and sliced celery.

Cook gently until soft but not brown, add flour, cook 2 minutes.

Remove from heat, gradually add milk and water; return to heat, add crumbled stock cube.

Cook, stirring, until mixture boils and thickens.

Add cream, white wine and salt and pepper to taste; stir in chicken, drained corn and drained mushrooms, heat through.

Toss breadcrumbs in extra butter in separate saucepan.

Pour chicken into greased ovenproof serving dish, sprinkle with grated cheese, top with buttered crumbs.

Bake in moderate oven 25 to 30 minutes.

Serves 4 to 6.

To prepare ahead: Prepare chicken mixture as described above, cool, refrigerate.

Next day, heat gently, pour into greased ovenproof dish, add topping, bake in moderate oven, as above.

Chicken à la King

1 lb. cooked, diced	½ cup cream
chicken	2 tablespoons dry
2 medium carrots	white wine
1 medium onion	½ red or green
10 oz. can cream of	pepper
mushroom soup	2 oz. mushrooms
	salt, pepper

Peel and slice carrots, cook in boiling salted water until barely tender, drain.

Combine soup, grated onion, cream, white wine, chopped pepper, sliced mushrooms and carrots in saucepan, bring gently to boil, stirring.

Cover, simmer 5 minutes.

Add chicken, stir over medium heat until heated through, add salt and pepper to taste.

Serves 2.

To prepare ahead: Prepare vegetables, dice chicken; cover separately, refrigerate.

Chicken Casserole with Almonds

3 lb. chicken, steamed	salt
¾ cup rice	1 cup mayonnaise
1 small onion	1½ cups diced celery
½ cup slivered almonds	4 hard-boiled eggs
10 oz. can cream of chicken soup	2 tablespoons lemon juice
10 oz. can cream of mushroom soup	½ cup fresh breadcrumbs
	1 oz. butter

Cook rice in usual way, drain. Remove meat from chicken, cut into cubes; chop onion and eggs.

Combine all ingredients except breadcrumbs and butter. Place mixture in large casserole, top with breadcrumbs which have been tossed in melted butter.

Bake uncovered 30 minutes in moderate oven. Serves 4 to 6.

To prepare ahead; Prepare as above, omitting breadcrumb topping; do not bake. Cover casserole with aluminium foil.

Refrigerate.

Remove from refrigerator 30 minutes before reheating; sprinkle topping over, cook 30 minutes in moderate oven.

Chicken with Mushrooms

1 lb. chopped cooked chicken	¼ cup milk
1 medium onion	4 oz. mushrooms
1 oz. butter	1 tablespoon chopped parsley
10 oz. can cream of chicken soup	

Heat butter in saucepan, add chopped onion.

Cook until tender but not brown, add sliced mushrooms.

Cook further 3 minutes.

Stir in combined soup and milk, add chopped chicken and parsley. Stir over heat until heated through.

If desired, toss 1 or 2 tablespoons slivered almonds in hot butter until browned, scatter on top of chicken.

Serve with noodles or rice or spoon on to hot toast.

Serves 2.

Oven-Fried Chicken

4 chicken pieces	4 oz. butter
½ cup flour	1 tablespoon chopped parsley
salt, pepper	

Dust chicken pieces with flour seasoned with salt and pepper.

Melt butter, pour into baking dish, arrange chicken pieces in dish close together, skin side down.

Cover with aluminium foil.

Bake in moderate oven 25 minutes.

Remove foil, turn pieces over and baste well with pan juices.

Cook, without foil a further 20 minutes or until chicken is tender.

Sprinkle with chopped parsley before serving. Serves 4.

To prepare ahead: Arrange chicken in melted butter as described above, cover, refrigerate. Then cook as above.

Chicken with Pineapple

3 lb. chicken (or chicken pieces)	1 oz. butter
1 onion	2 tablespoons flour
¼ lb. mushrooms	salt, pepper
¼ lb. bacon	½ pint water
15 oz. can pineapple pieces	1 chicken stock cube
	chopped parsley

Cut chicken into serving-sized pieces. Season 2 tablespoons flour with salt and pepper; toss chicken in this seasoned flour. Cut rind from bacon rashers. Divide each rasher into 3 pieces; roll each piece into a small roll and secure with a wooden stick. Slice onion and mushrooms.

Melt butter, fry bacon rolls and onion lightly, remove from pan. Fry chicken pieces until well browned on all sides, remove from pan. Add 1 tablespoon flour to pan and cook until brown (do not burn). Slowly stir in the water. Add crumbled stock cube. Bring to boil, stirring. Adjust seasoning if necessary.

Put mushrooms, onion, and chicken in casserole dish. Pour sauce over. Arrange drained pineapple pieces and bacon rolls (with wooden sticks removed) on top. Cover, cook in moderate oven 1 to 1¼ hours or until chicken is tender.

Serve in deep bowls with hot rice. Sprinkle with chopped parsley.

Serves 4.

Meat Dishes

Most of the dishes given here cook in minutes. In others, majority of the preparation can be done in advance, and we've added recipes for delicious casseroles which can be prepared ahead, and cooked, or reheated, when required

Little Carpetbag Steaks

4 pieces fillet steak, 1 in. thick	salt, pepper
1 bottle (10-12) oysters	lemon juice
	2 oz. butter

Sauce:

2 oz. butter	¼ cup dry sherry
2 tablespoons chopped parsley	1 teaspoon worcestershire sauce

Make small pocket in side of each steak, season with salt and pepper. Season oysters with lemon juice and pepper, place some in each pocket, secure with small skewers or wooden cocktail sticks.

Heat butter in frying pan, add steaks, cook until done as desired. Remove steaks from pan, reserve pan juices, keep steaks hot.

Sauce: Add butter to reserved pan juices, stir in sherry, sauce, and parsley. Add any juices from meat.

Bring to boil, spoon over steaks.

Serves 4.

Steak Diane

For each person:

8 to 10 oz. fillet steak	freshly ground pepper
3 oz. butter	½ clove garlic, crushed
1 tablespoon worcestershire sauce	1 tablespoon chopped parsley

Pound steak until it is quite thin. Season each side lightly with freshly ground pepper.

Put butter into pan; when sizzling, add steaks. While cooking on one side, rub garlic into top of steak with wooden spoon; turn steak over. Add worcestershire sauce to pan, swirl steak round in the pan juices.

When cooked to desired doneness, sprinkle with chopped parsley, transfer to heated plate.

A tablespoon of cream can be stirred into the sauce to soften the characteristic 'sharpness' of the sauce.

Steak with Brandy

4 pieces fillet steak	3 oz. butter
oil	½ cup brandy
pepper	2 tablespoons cream

Brush steaks with oil, sprinkle with freshly ground pepper.

Heat 2 oz. butter in pan, add steaks, cook until done as desired, remove from pan, keep hot.

Add remaining butter and brandy to pan; when butter has melted, stir in cream.

Do not allow to boil. Spoon sauce over steaks. Serves 4.

Steaks in Red Wine

2 oz. butter	6 shallots
4 thick fillet steaks	1 dessertspoon flour
½ oz. butter, extra	2 tablespoons red
1½ cups red wine	wine, extra
	salt, pepper

Heat butter in pan, add steaks, cook until browned and cooked to taste.

Remove steaks and keep warm.

Melt extra butter in pan, add chopped shallots, and cook 1 minute.

Add wine, cook quickly until liquid has been reduced to half original quantity.

Stir in flour which has been blended to smooth paste with extra wine. Season with salt and pepper.

Stir until sauce boils; boil 1 minute.

Return steaks to pan, spoon sauce over steak, serve immediately.

Serves 4.

Colourful curry accompaniments: papaw, sprinkled with coconut; finely chopped cucumber in yoghurt; pineapple with mint; chopped peppers; lemon wedges; fresh banana pieces.

Brandied Steaks Flambé

4 pieces fillet steak	2 oz. butter, extra
1 oz. butter	1 teaspoon chopped
1 tablespoon brandy	chives or parsley
2 tablespoons sherry	

Blend the 2 oz. butter with chopped chives or parsley; refrigerate to firm.

Pound meat until very thin (or ask butcher to do this).

Heat the 1 oz. butter; fry steaks quickly, turning once. Add brandy; when warm, set aflame; stir in sherry.

Top each steak with a pat of chive-butter; spoon sauce over.

Serves 4.

Steak Bordelaise

4 pieces fillet steak	1 tablespoon flour
1 onion	¾ cup red wine
2 shallots	butter for frying
salt, pepper	

Cook finely-chopped onion and chopped shallots in butter until onion is transparent.

Add steaks, cook on one side, season with salt and pepper. Turn, cook few minutes; stir in flour, then wine.

Cook, stirring, until sauce boils and thickens; cook until steaks are done to taste.

Serves 4.

Steak Au Poivre (Pepper Steak)

4 pieces rump, sirloin	¾ cup dry white wine
or fillet steak	1 dessertspoon brandy
2 tablespoons black	or dry sherry
peppercorns	½ oz. butter, extra
2 oz. butter	
1 dessertspoon oil	

Coarsely crush peppercorns, using rolling pin or mortar and pestle. You may need more peppercorns, depending on size of steaks. Press the crushed pepper into steak, or pound in with flat side of cleaver.

Let stand to absorb pepper flavour.

Heat butter and oil in pan, add steaks, cook quickly on both sides to seal juices. Then cook until done as desired.

Remove steaks to hot serving plates.

Stir into pan white wine and brandy or sherry.

Bring to boil, scraping the pan.

Remove from heat, stir in extra butter. Strain over steaks.

Serves 4.

Fillet au Poivre

2 2 lb. fillets beef	1-2 oz. cracked
oil	peppercorns
1 dessertspoon	
ground cardamom	

Brush fillets with little oil. Combine cardamom with crushed peppercorns, press on to fillets, coating thickly. Stand 30 minutes for steak to absorb pepper flavour. Bake in hot oven 10 minutes, reduce heat to moderate, bake further 15 to 20 minutes, depending on thickness of fillets. Cut fillets into thick slices, spoon sauce over.

Sauce: Remove all but 1 tablespoon drippings from baking dish, add ⅓ cup brandy, ⅓ cup sherry 2 oz. butter, ¼ cup finely chopped parsely; heat gently.

Serve fillets with glazed baby onions (parboil onions, drain, cook in butter, to which 1 teaspoon sugar has been added, until glazed and brown); and, if desired, young green beans.

Note: Amount of peppercorns will depend on how peppery you want the steak to be. If you're not sure of your guest's tastes, it might be best to use 1 oz. only.

Serves 6.

Sukiyaki

1½ lb. lean round	4 oz. chinese
steak	vermicelli (very
4 medium onions	fine transparent
2 medium carrots	noodles)
½ lb. green beans	½ cup sugar
½ medium cabbage	⅔ cup soy sauce
8 oz. can bamboo	1 cup sweet white
shoots	wine
2 tablespoons oil	1 cup water

Put steak in freezer for 2 hours until firm. With sharp knife, cut steak into very thin slices, approx. 3 in. long. Slice onions, slice bamboo shoots, cut carrots into fine straws about 2 in. long. String beans and slice about same size as carrots. Wash and shred cabbage. Put vermicelli, cut into 3 in. lengths, in bowl, cover with warm water, stand 10 minutes; drain. Arrange prepared ingredients attractively on large plate.

Heat oil in electric frypan or large frying pan. Add about ⅓ of the meat to pan, toss quickly until meat has changed colour, keeping it to one side of pan. Sprinkle over a little sugar, soy sauce, and wine. Add about ⅛ each of vermicelli, onions, carrots, beans, cabbage, and bamboo shoots, keeping each vegetable separate. Using chopsticks or fork, toss vegetables lightly so they cook evenly.

Sprinkle over a little more sugar, soy sauce, wine and water.

Do not overcook vegetables, they should be crisp when served. As sukiyaki is served from pan, don't try to cook it all at once; keep adding more of the steak and prepared ingredients.

If desired, serve with 1 raw egg, lightly beaten, for each person in individual small bowls. Dip sukiyaki into the egg; the heat of the meat and vegetables cooks the egg so that it sets in a light coating round each individual piece.

Continue until all ingredients have been used.
Serve with hot rice.
Serves 4.

Curried Minced Steak

1 oz. butter	1 tablespoon curry
1½ lb. minced steak	powder
1 large onion	1 tablespoon lemon
1 green apple	juice
2 tablespoons fruit	1 pkt vegetable soup
chutney	1 pint water
salt, pepper	

Heat butter in frying pan, add steak, stir constantly until meat changes colour.

Add peeled and chopped onion and apple, sauté until well browned. Add remaining ingredients, stir until mixture boils.

Reduce heat, cover, simmer 20 to 25 minutes, or until liquid is reduced and meat tender.

Serve with hot rice.
Serves 4.

Savoury Mince

1 oz. butter	½ teaspoon mixed
1 onion	herbs
1½ lb. minced steak	2 tablespoons flour
1 teaspoon salt	1 cup water
¼ teaspoon pepper	2 tablespoons
	tomato sauce

Heat butter in shallow frying pan, add chopped onion, steak, salt, pepper, and mixed herbs.

Stir constantly over medium heat until meat is well browned. Pour off any surplus fat.

Add flour, stir 5 minutes, or until flour is browned.

Gradually add water and tomato sauce, stir until mixture boils and thickens.

Reduce heat; simmer, uncovered, 10 to 15 minutes.

Serves 4.

Chilli Con Carne

1 dessertspoon oil	10 oz. can red
1 large onion	kidney beans
1 clove garlic	½ teaspoon chilli
16 oz. can tomato	powder
soup	salt
1 lb. minced steak	

Heat oil in saucepan, fry chopped onion, crushed garlic, and minced steak until steak is well browned. Pour off surplus fat.

Add undiluted tomato soup, chilli powder, and salt to taste.

Simmer gently 10 to 15 minutes or until meat is tender.

Add undrained kidney beans, heat through.
Serve with french bread and tossed green salad.
Serves 4.

Minted Lamb Chops

8 lamb loin chops	½ teaspoon sugar
2 oz. butter	1 dessertspoon
1 teaspoon grated	chopped mint
lemon rind	1 small onion
1 dessertspoon	
lemon juice	

Grill chops until tender. While grilling, prepare sauce: melt butter in saucepan, add finely chopped onion.

Sauté until tender; add lemon rind, juice, sugar, and mint, heat gently.

Spoon over hot chops.
Serves 4.

Herbed Chops

4 lamb loin chops	1 tablespoon oil
1 dessertspoon dried	salt, pepper
rosemary	1 dessertspoon
½ teaspoon thyme	finely chopped mint
1 dessertspoon lemon	
juice	

Trim any excess fat from chops, place chops on plate. Combine remaining ingredients, brush over both sides of chops.

Allow to stand 20 to 30 minutes before grilling.

Grill 10 minutes or until tender, turning once and brushing over with a little of the marinade during cooking.

Serves 2

Lamb and Bacon Casserole

1½ lb. lamb neck chops
½ lb. bacon pieces
1 large onion
½ green pepper
1½ tablespoons flour
salt, pepper
1 teaspoon worcestershire sauce
1 dessertspoon tomato sauce
¾ pint water
1 chicken stock cube

Fry bacon pieces and chopped onion lightly, remove from pan. Add chops to pan, brown well; add a little butter to pan, if necessary. When chops are browned on both sides, remove from pan.

Add flour to pan drippings, cook until brown; do not allow flour to burn. Add water gradually, bring to boil, stirring; add seasonings, sauces and crumbled stock cube. Put chops, onion and bacon in casserole, pour sauce over. Cover, cook in moderate oven 1½ hours. Add chopped green pepper for last 15 minutes of cooking time.
Serves 4.

Oriental Chops

6 lamb chump or short loin chops
2 shallots
⅓ cup soy sauce
½ cup water
1 chicken stock cube
1 tablespoon grated green ginger or
1 teaspoon ground ginger

Chop shallots, mix in bowl with soy sauce, water, crumbled stock cube, and ginger.
Add chops, marinate 1 hour.
Drain chops, grill, brushing occasionally with remaining marinade until tender.
Serves 3 or 6.

Lemon-Curried Chops

4 chump chops (or 8 short loin chops)
⅓ cup lemon juice
3 teaspoons curry powder
1 teaspoon salt
¼ teaspoon sugar
1½ oz. butter

Combine lemon juice, curry powder, salt and sugar; brush mixture over chops, let stand 30 minutes, or longer, for chops to absorb flavours.
Or cover, and refrigerate overnight.
Heat butter in pan, cook chops until brown and tender.
Serves 4.

Curried Sausages

2 tb. thick pork or beef sausages
1 teaspoon salt
3 tablespoons vinegar
3 oz. butter
2 onions
1 green apple
1 tablespoon curry powder
salt, pepper
¼ teaspoon mixed herbs
2½ cups water
2 chicken stock cubes
1 tablespoon flour
¼ cup water, extra

Put sausages into saucepan, cover with cold water, add salt and vinegar. Cover and bring to boil, reduce heat and simmer gently 10 minutes, drain.

Melt butter in frying pan, sauté peeled and chopped onions and apple for 5 minutes. Add curry powder, salt, pepper, and mixed herbs, stir over heat for 3 minutes. Add water and crumbled stock cubes, bring to the boil. Remove skins from sausages, cut in half lengthwise, add to curry, reduce heat, simmer 10 minutes. Blend flour and extra water, add to curry, stir until sauce boils and thickens.
Serve with boiled rice.
Serves 6.

Lamb Curry

1 oz. butter
1 large onion
1 clove garlic
salt, pepper
2 lb. lamb leg chops
1¼ tablespoons curry powder
½ cup tomato sauce
1½ cups water
½ teaspoon paprika
1 teaspoon cinnamon
1 teaspoon allspice
1 teaspoon mixed spice

Bone chops, remove any excess fat, cut into 1 in. cubes. Heat butter in frying pan, add peeled and sliced onion, crushed garlic, salt and pepper. Sauté few minutes, then add meat; brown well. Push meat to one side of pan, add curry, cook, stirring 3 minutes over low heat. Add tomato sauce, cook 5 minutes stirring constantly. Add water and remaining ingredients; mix well. Cover tightly, simmer gently 50 to 60 minutes or until meat is tender.
Serve with hot rice.
Serves 4.

Note: See page 27 for colourful accompaniments to curry.

Thai Pork—preparation is simple and cooking time is short for this superb dish, ideal for a buffet party. (See page 33.)

Sherried Veal

2 lb. veal steak	1 cup water
flour	½ cup dry sherry
2 oz. butter	1½ teaspoons
¼ cup oil	paprika
½ cup chopped	salt, pepper
shallots	¼ pint sour cream
¼ lb. mushrooms	chopped parsley
1 chicken stock	
cube	

Cut veal into very thin strips, toss in flour seasoned with salt and pepper.

Heat butter and oil in frying pan.

Add meat and brown well; remove from pan.

Add shallots and sliced mushrooms to pan, sauté a few minutes.

Return meat to pan with water, stock cube, sherry, paprika, salt and pepper to taste.

Simmer very gently 20 to 25 minutes, or until liquid has reduced by three-quarters and veal is tender.

Just before serving, stir in sour cream.

Sprinkle with chopped parsley and serve with hot, fluffy rice.

Serves 6.

Veal Marsala

1½ lb. veal steaks,	1 tablespoon
cut thin	chopped parsley
seasoned flour	2 oz. butter
1 egg	2 tablespoons oil
2 tablespoons milk	½ cup brandy
1 cup packaged dry	½ cup marsala
breadcrumbs	pinch oregano
½ cup grated	salt, pepper
parmesan cheese	

Pound steaks until thin, toss in flour seasoned with salt and pepper, dip in egg beaten with milk. Combine breadcrumbs, cheese and parsley. Press mixture firmly on to both sides of steaks.

Refrigerate 30 minutes.

Heat butter and oil in frying pan, add steaks, cook quickly on both sides until golden brown, reduce heat, cook slowly until tender, approximately 5 to 10 minutes.

Remove steaks from pan, keep hot. Drain excess oil from pan, add brandy, marsala, oregano, salt and pepper.

Simmer 2 minutes or until sauce is reduced slightly.

Spoon sauce over steaks.

Serves 4.

Veal with Almonds

1½ lb. veal steak	½ cup water
2 tablespoons oil	salt, pepper
3 sticks celery	2 tablespoons
8 oz. pkt. quick	cornflour
frozen beans	1 tablespoon soy
1 small red pepper	sauce
½ cup dry white	2 oz. slivered almonds
wine	

Cut veal into ¼ in. strips.

Heat oil and fry meat until browned, add sliced celery and pepper, cook few minutes.

Add white wine and water, frozen beans, salt and chopped pepper.

Simmer 5 to 8 minutes, remove from heat and add cornflour blended with soy sauce.

Return to heat, bring to boil, stirring.

Sauté almonds in a little butter until golden brown, scatter on top of each serving. Serve with hot rice.

Serves 4.

Veal Cordon Bleu

1½ lb. veal steaks,	3 or 4 thin slices ham
cut thin	3 oz. butter
salt, pepper	3 tablespoons oil
3 or 4 slices	flour
packaged swiss	1 egg
cheese	2 tablespoons milk
	dry breadcrumbs

Number of pieces of veal steak in 1½ lb. can vary, so we've given approximate numbers of slices of ham and cheese required. You'll need half a slice of swiss cheese and half a slice of ham for each piece of steak.

Pound steaks until very thin.

Season steaks with salt and pepper, press out flat. Put half a slice of swiss cheese over one half of each steak, top with a slice of ham, cut the same size as the cheese.

Fold steak over, secure with wooden cocktail sticks. Toss in flour, then egg beaten with milk, then breadcrumbs.

Refrigerate 30 minutes.

Heat butter and oil in frying pan, cook as for Wiener Schnitzel, but allow cooking time of approximately 20 minutes.

Serves 4.

Wiener Schnitzel

1½ lb. veal steaks, cut thin	2 oz. butter
flour	2 tablespoons oil
1 egg	1 dessertspoon lemon juice
packaged dry breadcrumbs	2 oz. butter, extra
	2 tablespoons milk

Press steaks out flat on board. Remove thin tissue from steak with sharp knife. Pound steaks with meat-mallet or rolling-pin. Toss steaks in flour, seasoned with salt and pepper.

Dip floured steaks into beaten egg and milk, until well coated on both sides.

Dip egg-glazed steaks immediately into dry breadcrumbs, covering both sides. Press crumbs on firmly with hand.

If possible, refrigerate 30 to 60 minutes, to firm the crumb coating so that crumbs do not fall off during cooking.

Combine butter and oil in frying pan, heat until butter is melted and begins to sizzle.

Add one steak at a time, so that the butter mixture retains the heat necessary to brown the steaks.

Cook quickly on both sides about 2 to 3 minutes; reduce heat, cook until tender, approximately 5 to 10 minutes, depending on thickness of steaks.

Use tongs when turning schnitzels during cooking; a fork would pierce the meat and cause the juices to escape. Schnitzels would be drier and less tender.

Remove steaks from pan, drain on absorbent paper.

Add extra butter and lemon juice to pan, heat, pour over steaks.

Serve with lemon wedges.

Serves 4.

Veal with Mushrooms

4 veal chops	8 small onions
¼ lb. small mushrooms	½ cup cream
boiling salted water	1 cup dry white wine
4 oz. butter	chopped parsley
	salt, pepper

Peel onions, keeping them whole; cook in boiling salted water 10 minutes, drain.

Heat butter in pan, add chops, cook until golden brown on one side; turn and cook on other side.

When done, remove and keep warm.

Add sliced mushrooms and par-boiled onions to pan, season with salt and pepper.

Cook until onions are golden brown, shaking pan occasionally. Stir in white wine, then add cream.

Cook a few minutes, stirring frequently; do not allow to boil.

Pour sauce over chops, sprinkle with parsley. Serves 4.

Note: For hearty eaters, or if chops are small, buy 8 chops.

Thai Pork

1½ lb. lean pork (4 large chops)	2 onions
2 tablespoons cornflour	4 tomatoes
⅓ cup oil	2 tablespoons soy sauce
1 clove garlic	2 tablespoons sugar
1 green cucumber	2 tablespoons vinegar
1 teaspoon finely chopped red or green chilli	½ cup water
	1 chicken stock cube

Remove rind and any excess fat from chops, cut meat into 1 in. cubes, sprinkle cornflour over. Heat 2 tablespoons oil in pan, fry pork until brown and tender; remove from pan. Add remaining oil, fry crushed garlic and peeled, sliced onions 5 minutes. Add unpeeled and chopped cucumber, skinned and chopped tomatoes, and finely chopped chilli, cover, cook 5 minutes. Add pork to vegetables. Combine soy sauce, sugar, vinegar, water, and crumbled stock cube, pour over pork and vegetables, bring mixture slowly to boil. Serve with hot rice.

Serves 4.

Orange Pork Chops

4 large pork chops	¼ teaspoon cinnamon
1 tablespoon oil	½ teaspoon salt
1 cup water	1½ dessertspoons cornflour
⅔ cup orange juice	½ medium orange
2 tablespoons brown sugar	

Cook pork chops in hot oil until well browned on both sides. Pour off excess fat; stir in water, orange juice, brown sugar, cinnamon and salt. Bring to boil, stirring; reduce heat, cover and simmer for 15 minutes, or until chops are tender.

Remove chops from pan; stir in cornflour which has been blended with a little extra water; continue stirring until sauce boils and thickens. Add thinly sliced orange and return chops to sauce; reheat gently. Serve with hot rice.

Serves 4.

Kidneys Bordelaise

2 onions	8 lamb kidneys
4 oz. mushrooms	1 tablespoon tomato
1 oz. butter	paste
1 cup dry white wine	2 oz. butter, extra
2 cups water	2 tablespoons flour
2 chicken stock	1 tablespoon
cubes	chopped parsley
salt, pepper	

Remove skin from kidneys, cut in half, and remove any fat and tubes. Soak in warm salted water for 20 minutes; drain and dry on absorbent paper.

Chop onions very finely, slice mushrooms.

Melt 1 oz. butter in saucepan, sauté onions and mushrooms until lightly browned.

Add wine, 1 cup water, and one crumbled stock cube, simmer until reduced to half quantity.

Stir in tomato paste, salt and pepper.

Melt extra butter in saucepan, sauté kidneys 8 minutes, remove from pan.

Add flour to pan, stir over heat 2 minutes; remove from heat.

Add remaining water and crumbled stock cube, stir until smooth.

Add the mushroom sauce, return to heat, and continue stirring until sauce boils and thickens.

Add kidneys, simmer gently 10 minutes.

Sprinkle with parsley, serve with rice or creamy mashed potato.

Serves 4.

Devilled Kidneys

8 lamb kidneys	1 tablespoon
4 oz. butter	worcestershire sauce
½ cup finely-	1 tablespoon dry
chopped parsley	sherry
1 small onion	salt
1 clove garlic	

Soak kidneys in lightly-salted water 20 minutes.

Chop onion, crush garlic. Wash kidneys, remove skin and fat, cut in half.

Heat butter in pan, add onion and garlic, sauté until soft but not brown.

Add kidneys, cook quickly on both sides.

Add salt, worcestershire sauce, sherry, and parsley, mix well.

Spoon kidneys on to hot toast, spoon pan juices over.

Serves 2 or 4.

Meatloaf with Barbecue Sauce

1 lb. sausage mince	salt, pepper
1 lb. minced steak	1 tablespoon
1 cup fresh	chopped parsley
breadcrumbs	1 egg
2 onions	½ cup milk
1 dessertspoon curry	½ cup water
powder	

Sauce:

½ cup water	1 teaspoon instant
½ cup tomato sauce	coffee powder
¼ cup worcestershire	1 oz. butter
sauce	2 tablespoons lemon
2 tablespoons vinegar	juice
¼ cup brown sugar	

Combine sausage mince, minced steak, breadcrumbs, finely chopped onions, salt, pepper, curry powder, parsley, and egg in bowl. Beat until mixture is well combined. Gradually add combined milk and water, continue beating until mixture is very smooth.

Shape meat mixture into a loaf, put in greased baking dish. Bake in moderate oven 30 minutes.

Remove from oven, carefully pour off any surplus fat; pour sauce over meatloaf, return to oven, bake further 45 minutes, basting frequently with sauce. Serve hot with vegetables or cold with salad.

Sauce: Combine all ingredients in saucepan, bring to boil, simmer 5 minutes.

Serves 4.

Lamb's Fry Casserole

1 lb. lamb's fry	2 rashers bacon
water	4 oz mushrooms
1 tablespoon vinegar	¾ cup water
flour	½ cup cream
2 oz. butter	salt, pepper

Soak lamb's fry in water and vinegar 15 minutes. Drain, and rinse, remove skin, cut into slices, wipe dry. Toss slices in a little flour, sauté in heated butter in pan until brown.

Add sliced mushrooms and chopped bacon, sauté 3 minutes. Add water and cream, season to taste with salt and pepper, simmer slowly, covered, 15 minutes.

Serves 4.

Note: If desired ¼ cup red wine can be added with the water.

Kidneys Bordelaise—kidneys cook to delicious tenderness in a rich, wine-flavoured mushroom sauce.

Desserts

Here are happy endings for any meal—recipes you can make in minutes, or prepare ahead and refrigerate or freeze until serving time. They're all delicious.

Chocolate Rum Mousse

4 oz. dark chocolate
4 eggs, separated
½ pint cream
1 tablespoon rum
extra whipped cream

Chop chocolate roughly, place in top of double saucepan.

Stir over hot water until melted.

Remove from heat, cool slightly, blend in egg-yolks one at a time.

Beat well until mixture is smooth and thick.

Fold in whipped cream, rum, then softly beaten egg-whites.

Spoon into individual glass serving dishes.

Refrigerate until firm.

Before serving, spoon Chocolate Rum Sauce over mousse, top with extra whipped cream.

Chocolate Rum Sauce: Blend well together ⅓ cup each of bottled chocolate sauce or chocolate topping and rum.

Serves 4.

Strawberry Mousse

1 punnet strawberries
1 dessertspoon water
1 teaspoon gelatine
2 egg-whites
½ cup castor sugar
1½ cups cream
1 tablespoon lemon juice

Wash and hull strawberries, mash well, (1 punnet should give approximately 1¼ cups pulp).

Add gelatine to water, stand 5 minutes.

Dissolve over hot water.

Beat egg-whites until soft peaks form, gradually add sugar, beating until dissolved. Whip cream until soft peaks form; fold into egg-white mixture.

Add strawberries, lemon juice and gelatine, fold in lightly.

Pour into wetted mould, or into individual serving dishes.

Refrigerate until set.

Serves 6.

Easy Chocolate Mousse

½ pint cream
1 to 2 tablespoons sweet sherry
2 tablespoons bottled chocolate topping
chopped nuts

Whip cream, fold in sherry. Then lightly fold through chocolate topping.

Place mixture into a freezer tray and half-freeze.

For serving, spoon into glasses, sprinkle with chopped nuts.

Serves 2.

Cold Grand Marnier Soufflé

4 eggs, separated
⅔ cup castor sugar
1 dessertspoon gelatine
2 tablespoons cold water
⅓ cup Grand Marnier
1 cup cream

Combine egg-yolks and sugar in top of double boiler; beat together, then stir over simmering water until thick, remove from hot water.

Soften gelatine in cold water, dissolve over hot water, cool. Beat into egg mixture, beating with wooden spoon until cold. Then beat in Grand Marnier.

Whip cream until stiff; beat egg-whites until soft peaks form.

Fold Grand Marnier mixture into cream, then fold in egg-whites.

Spoon into soufflé dish.

Refrigerate until set.

Decorate with whipped cream.

Serves 4 to 6.

Brandied Cream Pie

Cream Pie Shell

¾ pint cream
¼ cup castor sugar

2 tablespoons brandy
6 small coconut
  macaroons

Whip cream until stiff, fold in sugar, brandy, and crushed macaroons.

Spread evenly over sides and base of 8 in. pie plate lined with strips of aluminium foil (to ensure easy removal of shell after freezing).

Freeze 2 hours, or until firm.

Carefully remove foil from shell, put shell on serving dish; spoon in filling. If desired, pipe a decorative edge to pie with ¼ to ½ pint extra whipped cream.

Freeze for a further 1 hour before serving.

Filling: Any fresh or canned fruits can be used as a filling. Fresh strawberries, sprinkled with sugar, and brandy or grand marnier, are delicious. Or arrange canned pear slices in pie shell and spoon over caramel sauce.

Lemon Cheesecake

Crumb Crust:

8 oz. plain sweet
  biscuits

4 oz. butter

Filling:

8 oz. packaged
  cream cheese
14 oz. can sweetened
  condensed milk

2 eggs, separated
¼ cup lemon juice
1 dessertspoon
  grated lemon rind
½ cup castor sugar

Crumb Crust: Crush biscuits to fine crumbs. Melt butter, stir into crumbs, press into 8 in. springform pan, lining base and bringing crumb mixture halfway up sides.

Filling: Beat cheese in electric mixer, beat in condensed milk, lemon rind and juice, and egg-yolks; pour into prepared crumb crust.

Whip whites until stiff, gradually beat in half the sugar, beat until stiff, fold in remaining sugar. Spread evenly over filling.

Bake in moderate oven 5 minutes to brown the meringue.

Remove from tin when cold.

Pears with Coffee Cream

1 lb. 13 oz. can pear
  halves
½ pint cream
1 dessertspoon
  instant coffee
  powder

2 tablespoons brandy
⅓ cup castor sugar
½ teaspoon vanilla
¼ cup chopped walnuts

Drain pears thoroughly, (the syrup is not required in this recipe). Whip cream until thick; dissolve instant coffee in brandy, stir into cream with sugar and vanilla.

Spoon into freezer tray, cover with aluminium foil, freeze several hours or until required.

Just before serving arrange pear halves, cut side up; fill cavities with the coffee cream, sprinkle with chopped nuts.

Serves 4 to 6.

Tortoni

¾ pint cream
4 oz. coconut
  macaroons

½ teaspoon vanilla
1 tablespoon sherry,
  rum or brandy

Beat cream until thick, add the well-crushed macaroons and mix thoroughly; stir in vanilla and sherry. A few finely-chopped almonds can also be added.

Spoon into refrigerator tray, or into small individual containers.

Freeze just until firm.

This also makes a delicious topping for fresh or canned fruit.

If using as a topping, do not freeze.

Serves 4.

Lemon Gelato

1¼ cups sugar
½ cup lemon juice
4¾ cups water

2 tablespoons grated
  lemon rind
½ pint sour cream

In large saucepan place sugar, lemon juice, water and lemon rind. Bring slowly to boil, stirring until sugar has dissolved. Boil 15 minutes, strain; cool. When quite cold, stir in sour cream; pour into refrigerator trays; freeze.

When the cream is added to the lemon syrup, the mixtures do not immediately combine. However, while freezing, stir the mixture with fork frequently; the two mixtures soon blend together.

Serves 4 to 6.

Pineapple Soufflé

2 packets lemon jelly crystals	1 tablespoon lemon juice
1 pint boiling water	1 tablespoon dry sherry
15 oz. can crushed pineapple	¼ pint cream
	1 egg-white

Dissolve jellies in boiling water, cool, then refrigerate until beginning to set. Beat cream until thick.

Beat egg-white until soft peaks form; continue beating, gradually adding jelly. Beat until mixture is thick and creamy. Fold in lemon juice, sherry, drained pineapple, and whipped cream. Pour into large soufflé dish or deep serving dish, refrigerate until set. Serve with whipped cream.

Serves 4.

Pineapple Alaska

1 pineapple	2 egg-whites
canned fruit or fruit in season	pinch salt
icecream	½ cup sugar
	¼ cup brandy

Cut pineapple in half, lengthwise, including the green top. With sharp knife, remove fruit from shells, being careful not to pierce shells.

Remove core from pineapple, cut fruit into cubes or wedges; put into basin.

Add any fruit in season—mangoes, papaw, passionfruit, bananas which have been dipped in lemon juice to retain their colour. Cut fruit in similar size to pineapple pieces.

Sprinkle fruit with a little sugar, pour brandy over.

Cover bowl, let stand 30 minutes.

Just before serving time, fill fruit back into pineapple shells. Spoon very firm vanilla icecream over, cover with meringue, spreading meringue on to edges of pineapple to provide a firm seal for the firm icecream.

Put filled pineapple shells on to baking tray. Place in moderate oven 5 minutes to tint meringue. Some slivered almonds can be scattered over meringue before placing in oven.

Meringue: Beat egg-whites with salt until soft peaks form. Gradually beat in the ½ cup of sugar until of meringue consistency.

Pineapple Alaska can be made with small pineapples, so that each pineapple half provides an individual serving; or one large pineapple can be used and the dessert spooned from the shells to the individual serving dishes.

Melon Alaska

1 small rockmelon	1 passionfruit
2 tablespoons sweet sherry	1 egg-white
2 dessertspoons sugar	2 tablespoons sugar, extra
	icecream

Halve rockmelon, remove seeds. Sprinkle one tablespoon sherry and one dessertspoon sugar over each half.

Put passionfruit pulp in centre. Beat egg-white until soft peaks form, gradually add extra sugar, beating well after each addition.

Put a scoop of very firm icecream into centre of each melon half. Cover top of melon quickly with meringue, bringing it to the edges of melon.

Bake in moderate oven 5 minutes or until meringue is set and golden.

Serve immediately.

Serves 2.

Strawberries Romanoff

2 punnets fresh or 2 packets quick-frozen strawberries	½ cup brandy or cointreau
	1 cup cream

Sweeten fresh strawberries with a little sugar. Pour brandy or cointreau over. Cover until serving time.

Arrange in individual serving dishes, top with whipped cream. Or blend whipped cream with 1 small block of vanilla icecream which has been allowed to soften slightly.

Spoon over strawberries.

Serves 6.

Chocolate-Mint Icecream

4-oz. packet after-dinner chocolate mints	3 tablespoons cream
	1 tablespoon rum
	1 tablespoon water

Melt chocolate mints over hot water, stirring. Stir in water, cream, and rum.

Pour hot sauce over scoops of vanilla icecream.

Serves 3 to 4.

Rosé Wine Ice—a delicious summer dessert, light, and full of flavour; a perfect dinner-party dessert. (See page 40.)

Orange Sorbet

1⅔ cups bottled orange squash (approx. half 26 oz. bottle)	1⅔ cups water 1 egg-white 3 tablespoons brandy or grand marnier

Meringue:

1 cup sugar ⅓ cup water	¼ teaspoon cream of tartar 2 egg-whites

Combine water, orange squash, and unbeaten egg-white in deep 8 in. cake tin; whisk lightly. Freeze until partly frozen. Remove from freezer, fold into meringue with brandy; whisk lightly. Pour into cake tin, return to freezer, freeze until set, stirring occasionally with fork to blend mixture evenly.

To serve, flake lightly with fork, fill into glasses. **Meringue:** Place sugar, water and cream of tartar in saucepan. Stir until sugar is dissolved, bring to boil, rapidly boil 4 to 5 minutes; remove from heat. Beat egg-whites until soft peaks form. Pour the hot sugar-syrup into the egg-whites in a very thin, slow stream, beating steadily all the time. Serves 6.

Lemon Sorbet

Substitute lemon squash for orange squash. Add ¼ cup fresh lemon juice with the lemon squash. Omit brandy.

Tropical Fruit Salad

1 ripe pawpaw 3 mangoes 15 oz. can pineapple pieces 1 dozen strawberries	1 tablespoon orange juice 3 tablespoons brandy 2 tablespoons kirsch sugar

Remove seeds from pawpaw; cut peeled fruit into large dice.

Skin mangoes, cut into pieces.

Combine pawpaw, mangoes, and drained pineapple in bowl, sprinkle with little sugar, add combined orange juice and brandy.

Cover, let stand 1 hour.

Hull strawberries, cut in half. Put into small bowl, add kirsch.

Let stand 1 hour.

At serving time, gently combine all fruits with their liquids, spoon into serving glasses.

Top with whipped cream.

Serves 6.

Rosé Wine Ice

1 cup sugar 2 cups water	26 oz. bottle rosé wine

Combine sugar and water in saucepan, stir over heat until sugar dissolves, bring to boil, boil 5 minutes; cool.

Add rosé wine, pour into ice trays and freeze. Stir occasionally with fork until mixture has set through.

Fill into serving glasses.

Serves 6.

Brandied Oranges

6 oranges boiling water 1½ cups sugar	2 cups water ⅓ cup brandy

Peel oranges, removing every piece of white pith. Take the rind off 2 oranges, cut into very fine strips (use scissors to make this easier); use only the very thinly peeled orange rind, do not include any of the white pith, which has a bitter taste.

Drop orange strips into small saucepan of boiling water.

Cook 5 minutes; drain, run cold water over. This preliminary blanching removes any bitterness from orange rind and gives it a good colour.

Put sugar and the 2 cups water in saucepan, stir over gentle heat until sugar dissolves.

Add the strips of orange rind, increase heat; cook, stirring occasionally, until syrup thickens. Remove from heat, stir in brandy.

Put oranges in heatproof bowl, pour over hot brandied syrup and orange strips. Cool, refrigerate.

If preparing this the night before, cover dish with plastic food wrap; when cold, refrigerate.

Serve oranges with syrup and rind spooned over. Give guests small knife and fork for cutting and eating the orange, and spoon for the syrup.

A macaroon, sponge finger, or chocolate biscuit is a good accompaniment.

Note: For an even richer, more mellow flavour, substitute 4 tablespoons of any of the orange liqueurs—Grand Marnier or Curacao—for brandy in above recipe. Serves 6.

Brandy Alexander Icecream

¼ cup brandy
¼ cup Creme de
  Cacao
¼ cup cream

vanilla icecream
¼ pint cream for
  topping
1 oz. dark chocolate

Combine brandy, Creme de Cacao, and the ¼ cup cream in screw-top jar.

Refrigerate until ready to serve the dessert, then shake vigorously a few seconds to blend well.

To serve, spoon scoops of ice-cream into serving dishes, pour sauce over, top with whipped cream and grated chocolate.

Serves 4.

Pears Belle Hêlène

canned pear halves
vanilla icecream

canned or bottled
  chocolate sauce

For each serving, place one or two pear halves in serving dish. Top with a scoop of icecream. Pour over a little of the chocolate sauce.

Cherries Jubilee

16 oz. can cherries
1 tablespoon sugar
1 in. piece cinnamon
  stick
2 teaspoons
  arrowroot

water
½ cup brandy or
  cherry brandy
icecream

Drain cherries, reserving syrup. Pit cherries.

Combine cherry syrup, sugar and cinnamon stick in saucepan.

Bring slowly to boil, simmer gently 3 minutes, strain.

Blend arrowroot with a little water, stir into cherry syrup mixture.

Return to heat, stir until sauce boils and thickens. Add pitted cherries, heat thoroughly.

Add warmed brandy, ignite. Spoon sauce immediately over servings of vanilla icecream.

Serves 4.

Chocolate Rum Pie

Crumb Crust:

8 oz. plain sweet
  biscuits

4 oz. butter

Filling:

1 cup milk
3 oz. dark chocolate
2 eggs, separated
⅓ cup castor sugar

1 dessertspoon
  gelatine
½ cup hot water
½ pint cream
1 tablespoon rum

Crumb Crust: Crush biscuits finely, combine with melted butter; mix thoroughly. Press firmly over base and sides of 8 in. spring-form pan; refrigerate while preparing filling.

Filling: Place milk and roughly-chopped chocolate into saucepan, heat gently until chocolate is melted.

Beat egg-yolks and sugar until light and creamy in top of double saucepan.

Add hot milk and chocolate gradually, stirring until smooth.

Continue stirring over simmering water until chocolate mixture thickens; remove from heat, allow to cool.

Sprinkle gelatine over hot water, stir until dissolved; allow to cool.

Combine chocolate and gelatine mixtures when cool.

Refrigerate until mixture is cold and begins to thicken. Beat egg-whites until soft peaks form, add chocolate mixture, beat until well combined. Fold in whipped cream and rum.

Pour into crumb crust.

Refrigerate several hours or until firm.

For serving, top with extra whipped cream flavoured with a little rum; if desired, sprinkle with grated chocolate.

Lemon Delicious Pudding

2 oz. butter	2 tablespoons lemon
¾ cup castor sugar	juice
½ cup self-raising	1 tablespoon grated
flour	lemon rind
2 eggs, separated	1 cup milk

Beat softened butter and sugar until well combined, stir in sifted flour, lemon rind and juice.

Combine egg-yolks and milk, gradually add to mixture, beating well after each addition. Beat egg-whites until soft peaks form, fold carefully into mixture.

Pour into greased 3 pint ovenproof dish.

Bake in moderate oven approximately 35 minutes.

Serves 4.

Caramel Dumplings

1 cup self-raising	2 oz. butter
flour	2 to 3 tablespoons
pinch salt	milk

Syrup:

2 cups water	3 tablespoons
½ cup brown sugar	lemon juice
2 tablespoons	1 tablespoon grated
golden syrup	lemon rind

Sift flour and salt, rub in butter, add enough milk to mix to a firm dough.

Mould into 4 or 6 balls.

Combine syrup ingredients in saucepan, stir over heat until sugar dissolves.

Bring to boil, add dumplings, cover tightly and simmer 20 minutes.

Serves 4.

Caramel Bananas

2 oz. butter	4 large bananas
1 cup brown sugar,	¼ cup cream
lightly packed	pancakes

Peel and slice bananas.

Melt butter in heavy frying pan.

Add sugar, stir until sugar dissolves and bubbles. Add sliced bananas. Cook 3 minutes. Stir in cream.

Pour over pancakes.

Serve with whipped cream or icecream.

Serves 4.

Banana Fritters

½ cup plain flour	3 to 4 bananas
pinch salt	⅓ cup warm water
1 tablespoon oil	oil for deep-frying
1 egg, separated	

Sift flour and salt into bowl, make well in centre, add oil, egg-yolk, and water, beat well until batter is smooth.

Let stand at room temperature 30 minutes.

Beat egg-white until soft peaks form, fold into batter.

Peel bananas, cut in half, then half again lengthwise, coat in batter.

Deep-fry in hot oil until golden brown on both sides.

Lift on to kitchen paper, sprinkle with sugar.

Serve hot with cream or icecream.

Serves 4.

Note: To make Pineapple Fritters, substitute well-drained pineapple slices for banana.

Apple Fritters

3 to 4 green apples	½ cup milk
⅓ cup sugar	2 tablespoons brandy
¾ cup plain flour	½ oz. butter, melted
pinch salt	oil for deep frying
1 egg, separated	

Peel apples, leave whole and remove core, cut into ½ in. slices. Put in bowl, sprinkle with sugar, cover.

Sift flour and salt into bowl, make well in centre, add egg-yolk and milk, beat thoroughly until batter is smooth.

Add brandy and melted butter, beat well. Let stand 30 minutes.

Fold in softly beaten egg-white.

Coat apple slices with batter, deep fry in hot oil until golden brown on both sides, drain well.

Sprinkle with sugar, serve hot with cream.

Serves 4.

Brandied Oranges—delightfully fresh-tasting end to a meal. The perfect dessert to serve after curry. (See page 40.)

Pineapple Strudel

1 lb. packaged
  puff pastry
30 oz. can crushed
  pineapple
2 tablespoons sugar
1 dessertspoon
  lemon juice

2 tablespoons
  cornflour
½ cup pineapple
  syrup
2 tablespoons sugar,
  extra
2 tablespoons
  chopped almonds
1 egg, for glazing

Drain pineapple, reserve ½ cup of the syrup. Place drained pineapple in saucepan, add sugar, lemon juice and combined cornflour and pineapple syrup. Stir over heat until mixture boils and thickens, reduce heat, cook 2 minutes. Cool.

Roll pastry out on lightly floured surface, to approximately 33 in. x 9 in. Cut pastry into 3 even pieces 9 in. wide. Place an even amount of filling over one half and within 1 in. of the side, top and bottom edges of the 3 pieces of pastry. Glaze these edges with beaten egg and fold the second half of pastry over filling, press edges firmly together. Trim edges with a sharp knife.

Glaze top of pastry with beaten egg, sprinkle with combined extra sugar and almonds; make several slits in top pastry to allow steam to escape during cooking. Place on greased baking trays, bake in hot oven 20 to 25 minutes or until pastry is golden brown.

Serve with whipped cream.

Serves 6 to 8.

Note: Pineapple Strudel may be baked the day before required and stored in the refrigerator.

For serving, heat in moderate oven 10 to 15 minutes.

Apple Strudel

1 lb. packaged
  puff pastry
1 lb. 13 oz. can
  sweetened pie
  apple

2 tablespoons
  sultanas
3 tablespoons sugar
1 dessertspoon
  grated lemon rind

Combine all ingredients, except puff pastry; do not heat. Roll out pastry, then proceed with filling, folding and baking, as for Pineapple Strudel.

Serves 6 to 8.

Apple Crumble

4 green apples
3 tablespoons sugar

¼ cup water

Crumble Topping:

½ cup self-raising
  flour
½ teaspoon cinnamon

1½ oz. butter
¼ cup brown sugar,
  firmly packed

Peel, core and slice apples, place in saucepan with sugar and water.

Cover and cook over medium heat until apples are just tender; pour into oven-proof dish.

Crumble Topping: Sift flour and cinnamon into bowl. Rub in butter lightly, until mixture resembles fine breadcrumbs. Add brown sugar; mix thoroughly. Sprinkle crumble over apple.

Bake in moderate oven 25 to 30 minutes or until golden brown. Serve with cream or custard.

Serves 4.

Apple Sponge

4 green apples
3 tablespoons sugar

¼ cup water

Sponge Topping

2 oz. butter
¼ cup castor sugar
1 egg
½ teaspoon vanilla

1 cup self-raising
  flour
⅓ cup milk

Peel, core and slice apples, place in saucepan with sugar and water.

Cover and cook over medium heat until apples are just tender, pour into oven-proof dish.

Sponge: Cream butter and sugar, add vanilla and egg; beat well.

Stir in sifted flour alternately with milk.

Spoon mixture over hot stewed apple.

Bake in moderate oven 25 to 30 minutes, or until golden brown.

Serve with cream or custard.

Serves 4.

Dessert Omelet

Serves one

2 eggs
1 dessertspoon milk

½ teaspoon sugar
½ oz. butter

Separate eggs, beat yolks until thick.

Add sugar and milk.

Beat egg-whites until soft peaks form.

Fold whites into yolks.

Heat pan, add butter, turn pan to allow butter to flow evenly over base and around sides of pan.

Spread egg mixture evenly into pan.

Cook over medium heat until omelet puffs and under-part is lightly golden.

Bake in moderate oven 5 minutes, or place under hot griller until top is firm and springs back when pressed lightly with fingertips. Fill with any desired filling.

Fold over, serve immediately.

Strawberry and Cream Filling: Sweeten sliced fresh strawberries to taste, or use warmed canned strawberries.

Fill omelet with berries.

Fold over, decorate with whole fresh strawberries, or another spoonful of the canned strawberries.

Serve with cream.

Apricot Filling: Hot apricot jam, to which a little rum or brandy has been added, is another delicious filling or topping. Slivered toasted almonds can be sprinkled over.

Pancakes

1 cup plain flour
pinch salt

1 egg
½ pint milk

Sift flour and salt into bowl, make well in centre.

Add whole egg, work flour in from sides, add milk a little at a time.

Beat well until bubbles rise to surface; if possible, let stand 1 hour.

Heat pan, grease lightly. From small jug pour 2 to 3 tablespoons batter into pan, cook slowly, loosening edges with knife until set and lightly browned underneath.

Toss or turn, brown on other side.

Sprinkle with lemon juice and sugar.

Roll up and serve.

Makes 10 pancakes.

Banana Pancakes

4 bananas
2 oz. butter
3 tablespoons
  brown sugar

2 tablespoons brandy
pancakes

Peel bananas and cut in half lengthwise. Heat butter in frying pan, add bananas, sprinkle brown sugar over. Fry gently 3 to 5 minutes. Lift banana halves from pan and place in centre of pancakes; roll up. Return frying pan to heat, add brandy and continue stirring until sauce becomes smooth. Place rolled pancakes back into sauce, heat very gently. Serve with the sauce spooned over, and with whipped cream.

Serves 4.

Brandied Caramel Pears

1 oz. butter
1 lb. 13 oz. can pear
  halves
½ teaspoon
  cinnamon

2 tablespoons
  brandy
½ cup bottled
  caramel sauce
1 cup cream

Melt butter in frying pan, add cinnamon and drained pears. Saute pears until heated through, approximately 4 minutes. Add brandy, caramel sauce, and cream, stir until just simmering; remove from heat.

Delicious on their own, these Brandied Caramel Pears can also be served with icecream.

Serves 6.

Mocha Fudge Pudding

1 cup self-raising
  flour
pinch salt
¾ cup sugar
⅓ cup cocoa
½ cup milk

2 oz. butter
1 teaspoon vanilla
½ cup brown sugar,
  lightly packed
1 cup strong hot
  black coffee

Sift together flour, salt, sugar, and 2 tablespoons cocoa. Stir in milk, melted butter, and vanilla, mixing until well combined.

Spoon mixture into greased 3 pint ovenproof dish.

Combine brown sugar and remaining cocoa, sift over pudding mixture; carefully pour coffee over.

Bake in moderate oven approximately 50 minutes.

Serve with cream.

Serves 4.